PERMIAN

A Continuing Saga

ELMER KELTON

Edward C. Rowland, Executive Editor

*The Petroleum Museum wishes to thank the Abell-Hanger
Foundation, Midland, Texas, for the loan of the Tom Lovell and
other paintings for exhibit by the Museum and for permission to
use the Lovell paintings in this publication.*

Library of Congress Catalog Number 85-082165
ISBN 0-930380-18-5

The Petroleum Museum
1500 Interstate 20 West
Midland, Texas 79701

Printed in the United States of America

DEDICATION

The Permian Basin found, in George T. Abell, one of those rarest of men — one who is both a dreamer and a doer of deeds, a student of the past and a creator of the future.

He achieved success through hard labor, long hours, and the acceptance of risks. But he achieved more than mere business success. He also earned the respect and love of others for his honest modesty, the strength of his convictions, and his service as a civic leader in a variety of causes. As he often told friends, he felt that the land had been good to him, and he wanted to give something back.

George Abell's respect for the industry and for those in it — the entrepreneurs and leaders, the roustabouts and roughnecks in the fields, and the families who supported and helped them — inspired him to envision a monument built to it and to them.

Nowhere has his leadership proved more evident and fruitful than in the creation of this dream, the Permian Basin Petroleum Museum, by his service as its first president and on its board for many years.

This book is thus deservedly dedicated to George T. Abell, whose leadership and service has made the Permian Basin a far better place in which to live and work.

ACKNOWLEDGEMENTS

The Museum wishes to thank the Abell-Hanger Foundation, Midland, for the loan of the Tom Lovell and other paintings for exhibit in the museum, and for permission to reproduce the Lovell paintings in this book.

The Museum also wishes to thank its staff, especially Betty Orbeck, Museum Archivist; Jim Clark, Jim Clark and Associates, Scottsdale, Arizona; and Bobby Holt, Midland, for their assistance with this project.

Original portraits of the Petroleum Hall of Fame honorees were done by Gittings/Texas, Inc.; Gittings Western, Inc.; and by Rubin's Studio, Midland, Texas. Rubin's Studio also did all photographic restorations. Transparencies of the Lovell paintings were done by Archival Color, Inc., of New York, New York.

CONTENTS

INTRODUCTION

On this, the tenth anniversary celebration of the Petroleum Museum, it can truly be said that the Museum is a unique place, one that has perhaps surpassed even the dreams of its creators.

While this statement may seem self-serving, it certainly seems to be the opinion of the Museum's visitors, who never fail to leave impressed by what they have seen and learned. Travelers frequently remark that the Museum is the most interesting place seen on their trip. One travel writer, writing in the travel section of the *Daily News-Sun*, Sun City, Arizona, newspaper, stated it is "the most interesting museum I've seen outside of the Viking Museum in Oslo, Norway."

The attraction is the Museum's exhibits. The founders decided early on a policy of striving to be the best. To do so, they hired the finest exhibit designers available to create exhibits that are informative, attractive and, of utmost importance, involve the visitor. As a result, the Museum is able to boast of the world's largest walk-through marine diorama, the only full-sized indoor oilwell fire and a collection of historical paintings that people come back time after time to see.

How did such a remarkable place come to exist in a relatively small town in the middle of West Texas? The Museum was the brainchild of Midland oil and gas producer George T. Abell. His active campaigning gradually moved the idea from the Hotel Scharbauer coffeeshop (then a near-legendary site of the start of countless oil ventures) towards reality. In time, he called a meeting of interested men that eventually resulted in the Museum's charter as a non-profit institution in 1967. Five hundred forty petroleum industry leaders throughout the Southwest signed the petition for incorporation.

In 1969, Homer T. Fort was hired away from his job as head of Mobil Oil's public relations department to become the first director and to start fund-raising in earnest. Construction, carried out at a cost of $1.7 million, began in 1973. President Gerald R. Ford came from Washington to dedicate the building on September 13, 1975.

Expansion continued with the opening of the Archives Center and Library in 1979, and with the completion in 1981 of a wing to explain the process of petroleum production. Vice-President George Bush cut the ribbon at the dedication of the North Wing.

Today the Petroleum Museum stands as the largest and most complex petroleum-related museum in the world. Visitorship has averaged almost 50,000 per year, including travelers from over one hundred nations. Surveys have shown that the majority of visitors actually come from outside the Permian Basin, thanks to the Museum's location on Interstate 20.

The Museum tells two interrelated stories. The most obvious of the two is the technical story of the petroleum industry — how oil originated, how we look for it, find it, get it out of the ground, and how it affects lives in so many ways. Many of the exhibits use state-of-the-art electronics and lighting along with slide and video projectors, lifelike mannequins, and super-enlarged photographs.

The second story is that of the Permian Basin itself, a huge and varied chunk of land covering most of Western Texas and Southeastern New Mexico. The emphasis is on people, from the prehistoric man and woman of 10,000 years ago through the Spaniards, Comanches, ranchers and oilmen who have since moved through or populated the area.

This historical story is told through the Museum's most popular exhibit, a series of historical paintings (reproduced in this book) by artist Tom Lovell. The Lovell paintings, in particular, are truly remarkable in their ability to capture a moment of a historical event and to make it real. They go far beyond the limits of mere illustration to stand on their own as true works of art.

A museum must work not only to illustrate history but to preserve it. The Archives Center and Library serves to collect non-artifact historical materials (documents, books, photographs, maps, catalogs, etc.) chronicling the development of the petroleum industry in the Basin. In the up-to-date Center, located in the Museum, one can trace the development of the area's oil fields and of the equipment used to find and produce oil through the years. Special files include more than 6,000 photographs of area oil fields and boomtowns and over 600 tape recorded interviews with area industry pioneers.

The Museum also has an extensive collection, in addition to its displays, of petroleum and history-related equipment and artifacts. The study collections, which center on the 1920s, '30s and '40s, range from complete drilling rigs to individual pieces of costume jewelry.

An important part of the Museum's operations is the Santa Rita Club, the 175 member group of dedicated volunteers who staff the gift shop, serve as tour-leading docents, help in the Archives, and sometimes even don bluejeans and grab dustrags to help keep the exhibits sparkling. In the Museum's ten years of operation, Santa Rita members have donated over 80,000 hours of free service to the Museum.

What does the future hold for the Petroleum Museum? Now that the Museum's initial planned growth is complete, we are striving to become very much a part of the community through increased emphasis on new educational programs, lectures, traveling exhibits and outreach programs. Constant work must also take place to keep the Museum's exhibits maintained and up-to-date, both in appearance and content.

While no one can predict with certainty the future of the Permian Basin or of the petroleum industry, the Petroleum Museum will doubtlessly continue to tell both the technical story of the oil business and the events that make the Basin great.

Edward C. Rowland
Executive Vice-President/Director

TOM LOVELL, THE ARTIST

Tom Lovell spent four years researching and producing his fourteen historical paintings which grace the Permian Basin Petroleum Museum. This project was to alter his life and forever change the focus of his art career.

His work today is centered on the West, and he is regarded as a premier artist in the Western history field. He began life and career far from the West, however.

Born in New York City in 1909, he developed early in childhood a lifelong interest in history that would lead him naturally toward the type of work for which he has become famous. He recalls that even as a nine-year-old he was already giving himself to a love for history, "haunting" museums, sketching pictures of their artifacts, the utensils, the clothing, the weapons of people long gone,

daydreaming himself to faraway places and bygone times. He has never lost that youthful wonderment, that ability to carry himself away in imagination to the times and the places he paints, to live with and to know the characters who people his works.

Desire alone does not produce an artist. In his youth he worked at a variety of jobs. He was a deckhand on the S.S. Leviathan and learned firsthand the bitterness of winter in the North Atlantic. He worked for a pipeline construction company and was a messenger for Wright Aero Corporation, seeing with an artist's keen eye and storing in an artist's memory the details of everyday life for working men outdoors. Through this variety of enriching experiences he kept his sights trained always on his main goal, a full-time career in art. He was living in one of his country's most difficult times, the Great Depression, and he learned the faces of both joy and despair, faces that would appear again and again in the works of his later years.

In his junior year at Syracuse University's College of

Fine Arts he began illustrating pulp-magazine stories for seven dollars a drawing. That seemed big money for the times and gave him a professional status that made him the envy of his classmates. Pulp fiction concentrated upon action and movement, and the art had to convey a sense of drama compatible with the stories. The discipline of this genre taught him how to tell a story in pictures with simplicity and economy of line to complement the written word of such master pulp fictioneers as Max Brand, Walt Coburn and New Mexico's S. Omar Barker.

When he received packages of manuscripts from the magazine publishers, a fellow art student would often read them and help him decide what scenes to illustrate. That helper, Gloyd Simmons, became his wife and the mother of his two children, David and Deborah.

He moved, in time, from the pulp magazines to such prestigious and higher-paying "slicks" as *Cosmopolitan, Collier's, Ladies Home Journal* and *Woman's Home Companion.* He illustrated works by such popular writers of the period as Sinclair Lewis, Edna Ferber, Louis Bromfield and Paul Gallico. Because many of these stories were set in the past, he was able to indulge his lifelong interest in history as a complement to his professional art career. The story discipline of the pulps melded with the more sophisticated demands of the slick magazines to

broaden his challenges and hone his talents to a keener edge.

He joined the Marine Corps in 1944 with the hope of becoming a combat artist but instead was assigned to the staff of *Leatherneck Magazine,* official publication of the Corps. There he painted a broad range of both historical and contemporary Marine experiences, from Admiral Perry in Africa in 1830 to the struggle for Belleau Wood in World War I and the Battle of Guadalcanal in World War II. His painting of the Marines' landing on Tarawa hangs today in the main lobby of the Marine Corps Historical Center in Washington, D.C. While working on that scene he began a practice which he still uses today, constructing scale models of his subjects to help him with positioning and the effect of light and shadow.

When the war ended, he returned to illustrating major magazines. The National Geographic Society commissioned him to paint a series on the Vikings. His research, after reading all the historical material he could find, led him to Sweden, Norway, Denmark, England and Ireland to study backgrounds and further his basic knowledge. An example of his thoroughness was his analysis of a reconstructed Viking ship in Denmark, down to notes and sketches of the finest details and all its measurements. Back home, he built a scale model to assist him in bringing life and reality to his painting.

He painted a Civil War series for *Life* and a series on Mormon history for the Church of Jesus Christ of Latter-day Saints. In all of these assignments, his preliminary research was painstaking. Once that foundation was solidly built, he employed the imagination he had developed in boyhood to carry him back to time and place, putting himself into the scene so that it became alive and real, first to him, then ultimately to the viewer.

A turning point in his career was his selection in 1969 by the Abell-Hanger Foundation of Midland, Texas, to do the Permian Basin historical paintings which make up the body of this book. He approached this task with the same dedication and boundless curiosity which had characterized his earlier historical works. Initially he spent several weeks and drove eleven thousand miles visiting the West Texas and New Mexico sites of the incidents he was to recreate on canvas. During his four years of work on the project he returned periodically to the Basin to revisit the chosen places, study the available historical documents and talk to people who had lived some of the scenes he was painting. He learned the land, the topography, the soils and the plants. He watched and listened and studied the people of the Permian Basin, past and present, and he was deeply moved.

By the time he finished the project, he knew he wanted to devote the remainder of his career to the West and its history. In 1977 the Lovells moved from the shore of Long Island Sound in Connecticut to the piñon hills of Santa Fe, New Mexico. At one of the Southwest's great crossroads of history, he built a home and studio between the Sangre de Cristos and the Jémez Mountains. There he can sense the flow of history all around him. Inspiration is but a glance away.

In 1973 he was invited to exhibit at the National Cowboy Hall of Fame in Oklahoma City. He became a charter member of the National Academy of Western Art and in 1974 won its Prix de West Gold Medal. He is a member of the Society of Illustrators' Hall of Fame, inducted with N. C. Wyeth and Howard Pyle. He has been honored several times by the Cowboy Artists of America and by the Franklin Mint for individual pieces of work. His paintings hang in such places as the National Cowboy Hall of Fame, National Geographic Society, U. S. Maritime Academy, New Britain Museum, Syracuse University, The Explorers' Club and the headquarters of the New England, Continental and John Hancock insurance companies, as well as the Permian Basin Petroleum Museum.

One of the most widely-recognized of his works is a

painting of a Revolutionary soldier, used as a trademark in all Continental Insurance Company advertisements.

His works have a feel for the grand sweep of history, and though each is devoted to an individual incident or scene, a viewer senses the significance of this single thread to the larger tapestry.

His work on the Permian Basin series illustrates the special problems of the historical painter. He cannot share other artists' luxury of simply setting up his easel before the subject and recreating it from life. Not only are the people of the period gone, but often the landscape has radically changed. The historical artist lacks the luxury of the historical writer, who may omit details about which he is unsure.

"The writer may tiptoe through the minefields of doubt with a few well-chosen words, but the artist must stand and deliver," Lovell declares.

In the planning and execution of the Permian Basin paintings he worked particularly closely with George T. Abell, independent oil operator and Midland civic leader who had spearheaded not only the Abell-Hanger Foundation but the Petroleum Museum itself. Abell's help was particularly significant in the case of the painting of Captain John Pope's pioneer water-well drilling experiment near the Pecos River, because neither relics, drawings nor detailed descriptions of the drilling equipment could be found. Lovell first visited the original site in 1969 with local history buffs. The place was reached by pickup in a ranch pasture far from any improved road. While the artist studied the land and reconstructed the original scene in his mind's eye, one of the guiding party members scouted around with a metal detector, turning up long-lost percussion caps and rusted pieces that remained from Pope's boiler.

Pope's records were meticulously detailed in many respects but very sparse in regard to the equipment. From fragments of surviving records and Abell's lifelong knowledge of drilling, the two men painstakingly and over a long period of time managed to complete a cardboard model and perspective drawing that Lovell could use in re-creating the steam drilling rig as the painting's centerpiece.

Each painting was preceded by preliminary charcoal drawings and small color sketches of details, then a full-sized charcoal drawing to work out the perspective and placement of figures. As has become Lovell's practice, he built scale models and cardboard figures to help him with composition and lighting.

In the case of the Cabeza de Vaca painting, he consulted a doctor to determine the most likely way de Vaca would have operated upon a wounded Indian to remove an embedded projectile point. De Vaca's journal stated only that he did it, not *how* he did it.

The explorer Coronado required extensive research. A contemporary account states that Coronado wore a suit of golden armor, which seems unlikely. Study of records and museum exhibits convinced Lovell that the armor was of blackened steel inlaid with golden designs. Examples of authentic Spanish armor from that period are very scarce, and Lovell made detailed sketches and measurements of those he was able to find, recreating them first in cardboard before committing them to canvas.

Asked why he chose to do a painting of old Santa Fe, though that city is some distance from the Permian Basin, Lovell explained that it was a vital point in Southwestern history, and much that happened in the early days of the Basin had its origins there. Besides, he added with a laugh, using Santa Fe as a subject gave him an opportunity to paint one snow scene in the series.

Tom Lovell has come far from the days when he sketched black-and-white action drawings for pulp magazines at seven dollars apiece. His paintings today often sell in six figures. But he has never strayed from the lessons the pulps taught him about making a picture tell a story. Each is a captured moment of history in which people are *doing* something, reacting to something. Each draws the viewer into the scene, as the painter himself has been drawn, to witness the event, to share in the emotions of the characters, to wonder what has brought the incident about and what is to follow as a consequence. The viewer is subtly invited to use his own imagination and carry the story forward beyond the point at which the artist has left it.

Lovell combines the painstaking accuracy of the historian with the creativeness of the storyteller and the highly-polished craft of the classical artist to bring the past to vibrant life and to draw us into its reality for at least a little while. He has a rare ability to look upon a scene as it is now and see it in his mind as it must once have been. Even more important, he has the ability to show us what he has seen.

ELMER KELTON, THE AUTHOR

Elmer Kelton, who wrote the text for this collection of Tom Lovell's Permian Basin historical paintings, is a lifelong resident of the Permian Basin. He was born in 1926 at Horse Camp on the Five Wells Ranch in Andrews County, where his father and grandfather were both cowboys for Scharbauer Cattle Company.

His father, Buck Kelton, moved the family in 1929 to the McElroy Ranch in Crane and Upton counties, where the elder Kelton was first a cowboy, then a foreman and eventually manager, remaining on the ranch thirty-six years. Crane, in its third year of life when the Kelton family moved there, was still a classic example of the oilfield boomtown, made up largely of tents and frame "shotgun" houses, sheet-iron business buildings and dirt streets. It had a mobile but mostly conservative and God-fearing population; the singing always seemed stronger on Sunday morning than the shouting on Saturday night.

Though he grew up among some of the best cowboys who ever came out of West Texas, Kelton's own cowboy proficiencies were limited, and he began turning early in life toward a writing career. He attended Crane schools, then went to The University of Texas at Austin to major in journalism.

World War II intervened, and he went into the army, going to Europe as a combat rifleman whose rank never went beyond private first class. While stationed in Austria shortly after the war, he met Anna, who was to become his wife. After earning his bachelor's degree in journalism, he was hired by the *San Angelo Standard-Times* to become a farm and ranch reporter because of his West Texas background. He remained with that newspaper fifteen years, spent nearly five years editing *Sheep and Goat Raiser Magazine* for the Texas Sheep and Goat Raisers' Association, and since 1968 has been associate editor of *Livestock Weekly* in San Angelo.

His ambition since boyhood had been to become a novelist. He has conducted two careers in parallel: one as an agricultural writer, the other as a fiction writer. Like Tom Lovell, the artist, he began his professional career in the pulp magazines. Kelton sold his first Western short story during his senior year at the University in 1947, but only after writing many stories that were summarily rejected. Gradually he built magazine fiction writing into a steady sideline to his newspaper work.

His first novel was *Hot Iron*, published by Ballantine Books in 1955. Since then he has written and published twenty-six novels. Four have won Spur Awards from Western Writers of America as best Western novel of the year: *Buffalo Wagons* in 1956; *The Day the Cowboys Quit* in 1971; *The Time It Never Rained* in 1973; and *Eyes of the Hawk* in 1981.

Two of his novels have won the Western Heritage Award from the National Cowboy Hall of Fame: *The Time It Never Rained* and *The Good Old Boys*. Readers' Digest Condensed Books published shortened versions of *The Good Old Boys* and *The Wolf and the Buffalo*. Texas Christian University Press has recently reprinted *The Time It Never Rained* and *The Good Old Boys* for academic use.

In 1981 he wrote the text for a book of Western art by noted artist Frank McCarthy for the Greenwich Press.

Kelton continues to live in San Angelo, keeping both of his writing careers near the Permian Basin soil which has always been his inspiration.

He and Anna have three children: Gary of Plainview, Steve of Robert Lee and Kathy of San Angelo.

HISTORY OF THE PERMIAN BASIN

*T*he geologic formation which gives the Permian Basin its name lies sealed in subterranean darkness far beneath the surface, hidden from human eyes. It is an ancient sea floor from the Permian Age of more than two hundred million years ago, buried in later ages by thousands of feet of rock, shale and other deposits, then submitted to twisting and buckling by earth forces and to climatic changes that drastically altered the face of the land. The Basin remains, but above it lie a hundred thousand square miles of widely differing terrain in West Texas and Southeastern New Mexico, from the edge of the high plains in the north to the semi-desert cactus lands in the south and southwest. The surface is so varied in topography, soils and even climate that few observers considered an unseen common denominator until oil exploration in the 1920s began to delineate the Basin's outlines and bring its buried secrets to the light.

Man's history has represented but a few fleeting moments late in the Basin's long day. Painter Tom Lovell has chosen fourteen fragments out of that history to represent man's effect upon this unique place in the world, and the effect of this singular environment upon the men and women who left their footprints there.

Carbon dating of human bones shows that man was in the region at least ten to fifteen thousand years ago. How much farther back his tenure may extend is as yet unknown. It was a different land when man first ventured into the Basin. It was wetter and greener in the wake of the last Ice Age, and early men armed with spears and clubs and throwing sticks hunted animals doomed to extinction thousands of years ago by a drying climate and diminishing food resources. Many of the Basin's original creatures were unable to adapt, but man adjusted his lifestyle to the gradual alterations in his environment.

It is probable that the first Europeans to set foot upon today's Permian Basin region were Spaniard Cabeza de Vaca and three companions, treading their slow and uncertain way westward in 1535 after escaping from six years of captivity among Gulf Coast Indians. Like most newcomers who would follow after them through the next four hundred years, they saw the Basin only as a challenging obstacle that must be crossed en route to somewhere else. De Vaca sought others of his own race so that he might end his long exile and escape an exotic land far different from any he had known. Later Spanish adventurers such as Coronado sought gold and other riches, not a permanent home. They began the gradual and painful process, however, of dispossessing the primitive peoples who *had* made a home in the Basin through generations beyond counting.

On the east banks of the Pecos, they found Jumano Indians hunting buffalo afoot, using dogs as beasts of burden to carry packs and drag their belongings from one campsite to another. The Jumanos basically accepted the land as they found it, living from the plants and animals it furnished, however sparse these might sometimes be. By and large, the Indians who lived in or roamed over the Basin region were not farmers; they were hunters and gatherers. Some planted limited crops near the water, and others might occasionally burn the range to manipulate the movement of game, but in general they made little effort to alter the land for their own convenience. The mark they left upon it was small, and traces are difficult to find today. Old campsites are still occasionally discovered, as are caves in which the ancients took shelter. But by and large they subsisted upon what they found and built only with what nature provided. The earth has long since reclaimed what they borrowed from it.

Lovell represents those early peoples in a painting of peaceful nomads packing salt away from Lake Juan Cordona, and in a re-creation of old Pecos Pueblo, not far northwest of the Basin's western fringe, before the white man appeared to begin the brutal process of wresting the land from them. The first introduction of Spanish influence is shown in paintings of Cabeza de Vaca the healer and Coronado the explorer and despoiler.

A number of Spanish expeditions tracked across one part or another of the Basin in those questing years, headed by men like Antonio de Espejo in 1583, Gaspar Castaño de Sosa in 1590, Hernán Martín and Diego del Castillo, Diego de Guadalajara and Juan Dominguez de Mendoza of the next century. These were searchers, not settlers, though usually they were accompanied by crucifix-carrying priests who made an effort to convert the Indians to Christianity even while sword-carrying soldiers converted them to slavery. Like the Indians, the Spaniards left little physical mark which can be found in the Basin today. Their permanent missions were farther east or farther west. But they left a legacy of hatred among the Indians which carried forward into later times to other settlers from other lands.

Anglo acquaintanceship with the Basin began in the early 1800s. By this time Spain's hold on its Mexican colonies was weakening, and Mexico was chafing to cast off the yoke of Spanish rule as the United States had torn away from England. Some of the first Americans to traverse the Basin did so in search of new Mexican trade routes that might bypass the tariff collectors. They found and followed ancient Indian trails across the Pecos and into the Big Bend region. These explorations were generally unsuccessful from the standpoint of their original intent but developed a base of knowledge about the area that would eventually prove of much value.

Soon after Mexico threw off Spanish jurisdiction, Texas fought free of Mexican rule and established itself in 1836 as an independent republic. Its 1845 annexation into the United States was opposed by Mexico, leading to the Mexican War and Mexico's eventual loss not only of Texas but of New Mexico, Arizona and California. That brewing conflict and the twilight of Mexican dominance is depicted in Lovell's painting of Santa Fe in its final months under Governor Manuel Armijo. Americans' acquisition of Mexican California would lead to ambitious exploration of the Permian Basin shortly afterward in response to the discovery of gold at Sutter's Mill.

The California Gold Rush prompted heavy use of southern trails across the desert part of the Basin. A mile in those times was a distance to respect. Emigrants toiled weary miles and weary days trying to traverse an inhospitable region that offered them little comfort but much

resistance, even hostility. Horseback and wagon travelers found the Pecos River a far more formidable obstacle than it appears today, and the several routes that developed were dictated by its few passable fording points. The most famous of these fords is dramatically depicted in the Lovell painting of a difficult passage at Horsehead Crossing.

Captain Randolph Marcy quartered westward from Fort Smith, Arkansas, to Santa Fe in 1849 on a mission of exploration for a better route to California. Returning to Fort Smith, he passed near the present sites of such Basin cities as Monahans, Odessa, Midland and Big Spring. Some of his route is paralleled by Interstate 20 today.

Westward expansion was rapid in the fifteen years between the Mexican War and the Civil War. Americans believed strongly in what was known as Manifest Destiny, a divine obligation to expand the nation all the way from the Atlantic to the Pacific to accommodate its growing millions and bring all of it to the perceived degree of civilization already achieved in the East. The dream of a transcontinental railroad gave impetus to a more intensive exploration of the Basin in search of water supplies along the potential route. A result in 1854 was Captain John Pope's reconnaissance of the Permian Basin and the beginning of three years of deep drilling experiments. Failure dogged his ambitious efforts at producing water but earned him a place in history as the first of many who would drill through the Basin's unpromising surface crust and reach deep for the hidden wealth below. One Lovell painting centers around Pope's final drilling project near the Pecos. Ironically, in view of Pope's valiant efforts, it was to be thirty years before the dreams of a railroad through the region were transformed into reality, for a great war lay ahead, to be followed by a long and difficult period of reconstruction.

An interesting sidelight to history is the camel experiment long promoted and finally brought to fruition by Secretary of War Jefferson Davis in 1856. An interesting and technically successful trial to supplement horses and mules on the western deserts, the effort sent long-striding camels on more than one trek across the Permian Basin's water-shy mesquite and greasewood country in the late 1850s. But for unfortunate timing, just before the outbreak of war, and for Davis' adherence to the ill-starred fortunes of the Confederacy, the experiment might have led to broadscale use of the desert dromedaries in the Basin and beyond. Instead, it became merely a footnote rather than a chapter in Texas and Southwestern history.

The warrior Comanche and to a lesser degree the Apache were the most potent human barriers to settlement of the Basin. One legacy from the Spanish had been that through them the Indian acquired the horse, and the horse gave the Indian a mobility that transformed him from a troublesome but manageable foot soldier to a formidable adversary. A Lovell painting presents the Comanche at the zenith of his power, when he was unexcelled as a cavalryman. The Comanche was at war with Anglo Texas for some forty years, using the horse with deadly effectiveness as a weapon of war. He successfully thwarted serious white efforts to set down permanent roots in the Basin until he was defeated and set afoot by Colonel Ranald Mackenzie's troops on the high plains in 1874. Ironically, the last war chief of the Comanches was half white. Quanah Parker was the son of a chief, Peta Nocona, and a white captive, Cynthia Ann Parker, taken by the Comanches in 1836.

The Apache remained a threat in the western edges of the Basin through the rest of the decade. Black troops and their white officers out of Fort Davis fought a pitched battle with Apaches near Eagle Springs as late as July 30, 1880. Apache hostilities in the Basin subsided after the death of the unyielding Chiricahua Chief Victorio in the fall of that year.

Even when the Indians were gone, settlement did not come swiftly. The Basin's early permanent settlers were primarily ranchmen and cowboys. Most brought cattle, but some brought sheep, which despite their small size and apparent vulnerability to all hazards developed a formidable reputation for lifting mortgages. It did not take ranchmen long to discover why buffalo had always been short in number west of the Pecos River; it was a question of grass, or the lack of it. Stockmen quickly learned that drouth was more a steady boarder than an occasional visitor. Many brought old working methods and old stocking rates based on experiences in rainier regions to the east. The Basin proved to be an unyielding master, forcing modifications that fit the harsh realities of topography and climate. In the Trans-Pecos area especially, ranchmen would learn through bitter experience that cattle thrived best when they did not see each other often or in large numbers. Ranches tended to be large because so many acres were required to sustain a grazing animal.

By the same token, farmers had to alter both their methods and their expectations, brought out of more benign environments. The Basin was a stern land which had to be met on its own terms. For those who could not or would not change, the inevitable outcome was ruin. Farmers forced plowpoints into deep and fertile soil along the few rivers and streams, but most of their dryland efforts came to grief in a land plagued by long spells when it forgot to rain and by high, dry winds that could sweep up the topsoil and carry it aloft, higher than a bird could fly. All too often the sky turned a deep brown, occasionally almost a nighttime black, and a fragile soil

gradually bled away.

Nature's lessons were learned slowly and at great cost. For many who found the tuition price high, the discovery of oil in the Permian Basin was a Godsend.

Until oil, the Basin remained only sparsely populated. Most of its towns lay either on the Texas and Pacific Railroad, built along much the same route examined by Pope thirty years earlier, or were county seats surviving principally from farm and ranch trade and official courthouse business. These towns were connected by the steel rails and by a cobwebbing of twin-rut dirt roads worn deep into the prairie and desert soil by iron-rimmed wagon wheels and by the narrow tread of early automobiles. Distances were formidable. Tackling them was not a thing lightly undertaken. Lovell's painting of the mail car between Midland and Carlsbad illustrates the slow pace of the times, the feeling of isolation upon a broad, treeless land and under a big, open sky.

By the 1920s, drilling had become commonplace across the Permian Basin, but most wells were relatively shallow, their purpose to provide water that would make the land livable and productive despite the scarcity of rivers and streams. Artesian water wells were developed near Artesia and Roswell, New Mexico, Pecos and Toyah, Texas. The drillers of these wells were following in the footsteps of John Pope, a man ahead of his time.

A number of these early wells produced signs of oil and gas, but they caused little excitement because of their isolation and the lack of a market for their relatively light production. Presence of oil was often considered bad news when a rancher needed water for his cattle or a farmer needed it for his crops. The best use found for some of the early oil was in greasing windmills so the water could keep pumping. In faraway Titusville, Pennsylvania, however, a man named Edward L. Drake had pioneered a new industry by bringing in a shallow well at just short of seventy feet, hand-pumping eight or ten barrels of oil a day. The feat had created little general excitement at the time, but after development of the internal combustion engine, the nation was never to be the same.

At the turn of the century the value of oil started to rise along with increasing production of the automobile, and any show of oil began to be taken seriously. In 1903, a shallow field commenced development northwest of Toyah and produced modestly for more than twenty years, encouraging a flurry of activity in Reeves and Pecos counties. Most of this early effort yielded little except disappointment. Later developments would show that these early drillers simply did not explore deeply enough. They were limited by finances and the technol-

ogy of the times. The Basin became known as a "wildcatter's graveyard," a galling disappointment in view of the great oil booms set off farther east by the first big Texas discovery of Spindletop and the fields developed around such places as Sour Lake, Electra, Burkburnett and Ranger.

The Basin's first real commercial strike was far distant from its initial western efforts. The Underwriters Abrams No. 1 well (T. & P. Land Trust) was at the extreme eastern edge of the Basin in Mitchell County. In June, 1920, a significant oil deposit was struck at 2,410 feet in the Permian formation on railroad land. Though disappointing as a producer, it spurred other exploration and development in that area. Production remained modest overall, and the Mitchell County boom never materialized on the scale that boosters had hoped.

A wildcat gamble far to the southwest in Reagan County was to give the Basin its first real boom three years later. The discovery well was on University of Texas land, as were hundreds more that followed over the years. Almost eighty years earlier, the Republic of Texas had sought to promote education by designating millions of acres of land to the schools. In 1883 the newly-formed University of Texas was granted large areas in the underdeveloped region that would eventually become known as the Permian Basin. In the earliest times the land was deemed worthless because various Indian tribes forcibly disputed the deed. Even after the Indians were removed it was still considered of value only for grazing and brought relatively small revenues to the University.

In 1919 a Big Lake attorney, Rupert P. Ricker, and his associates applied for drilling permits on 431,136 acres of University land in the Permian Basin counties of Crockett, Reagan and Upton. He soon found he could not raise the filing fee of 10 cents an acre ($43,136) before the 30-day expiration date. He sold his and his associates' rights to Frank T. Pickrell and Haymon Krupp of El Paso who formed the Texon Oil and Land Company, a Delaware corporation, through which to operate. On January 8, 1921, the final evening before the permits were to expire, Pickrell and his crew hurriedly drilled a water well in Reagan County to hold their rights. The actual test well on University land was not spudded in until August 17 at a site just north of the Orient Railroad tracks, 13 miles west of Big Lake.

At the request of some Catholic women in New York who had invested in the venture, Pickrell christened the well "Santa Rita" after the Patron Saint of the Impossible. And it must have seemed impossible at times that the well would ever be completed. Twenty-one slow, monotonous months passed. Driller Carl Cromwell and his wife, living in an unpainted frame shack at the site, planted a garden and raised chickens. The Lovell painting of a bride's home at a wildcat well is indicative of the isolated life lived by the Cromwells and the many who would follow them. Cowboy drilling crews came and went, and the work doggedly went on. Then, on the morning of May 28, 1923, oil suddenly spouted through and over the eighty-four-foot wooden derrick. An incredible excitement followed. Crowds came by rail, automobile and wagon to watch the spectacle of oil and gas bursting periodically from the 3,050-foot hole, vaguely reminiscent of Old Faithful in the Yellowstone.

What had happened before was simply prelude. From that spring day at Santa Rita No. 1, the Basin's oil rush was on.

All was not easy, despite the initial euphoria. Isolation from existing fields created special problems in the procurement of equipment. It took a month, for example, to get pipe to carry the oil into storage tanks. Even that was but a temporary answer; a pipeline would be needed as more oil production was developed. One well does not make a field, and the next several drilled in the area were disappointingly weak. Not until No. 9 came in was the promise of the first well fully borne out.

The village of Big Lake, population two hundred when Cromwell had spudded in, became field headquarters for the region's feverish drilling activity. Best, four-and-one-half miles east of the well, for a time became home to five thousand restless people and quickly gained a wicked reputation for boomtown lawlessness. By contrast, Texon, built across the railroad tracks from the discovery well, was a company town where respect for law was a condition for staying.

The first pipeline was undertaken at Pickrell's instigation by Benedum and Trees of Pittsburgh. The Big Lake Oil Company was formed, seventy-five percent of its stock held by "the great wildcatter," Michael L. Benedum. Humble built an eight-inch pipeline which carried 20,000 barrels a day to a station near Ranger, from which it flowed ultimately to a Baytown refinery.

Driven by the impetus of the Reagan County discoveries, geologists quickly spread across the Basin, searching for surface manifestations of underground formations that might indicate deposits of oil and gas. Lovell's painting of the plane table party on King Mountain near McCamey is representative of this new kind of pioneer, using modern technology to make an intensive study of lands passed over for centuries by explorers, trailmakers and travelers who had found little to hold their interest. The geologists were followed by company landmen and enter-

prising speculators eager to slice a piece of this new pie for themselves. Big-money operators set up offices to trade in oil leases, shares and town lots. Little operators traded at curbside, if there were any curbs. The *Saturday Evening Post* termed the region "the oil Klondike."

Ranchers and farmers who had struggled for years against the challenge of dry skies and volatile markets found these newcomers both nuisance and salvation. Some ranchers like J. A. Slaughter of Post, featured in Lovell's chuckwagon scene, hopefully invited geologists to inspect their lands. For many, it was already too late. Midland County, for example, had lost a third of its population because of a drouth and a slump in agricultural and livestock prices that followed World War I. Upton County had lost half of its population since 1910.

Stories are legion – and some are true – about drillers strapped for cash, offering their crews stock in lieu of wages. Some workers accepted and shared in either the wealth or the disappointment. Others declined and lost out on fortunes. Stories are legion also about ranchers and farmers saved from bankruptcy by the timely arrival of a landman, or by a well that came in just ahead of the foreclosure notice.

In eastern Pecos County, Ira G. Yates and his wife Ann had struggled for years to make a ranch among rugged, rocky hills along the Pecos River. One story goes that the Mid-Kansas and Transcontinental had jointly drilled three dry test holes in the Basin and had resolved only after strong persuasion by geologist Frank R. Clark to make just one more try. That final gamble, on the Yates ranch, was destined to bring in one of the biggest producers in Basin history October 29, 1926, which happened to be the ranchman's 67th birthday. Distrusting the well's lasting quality, Yates sold about $180,000 in leases before the day was out, some to men who spent the night in a big red barn which he later converted into a rooming house to serve men working in the rapidly-growing Yates field. A town was founded nearby and was given the combined names of Yates and his wife: Iraan.

A splendid example of the "last-minute rescue" story was that of Thomas G. Hendrick, who ranched in Winkler County but had lost part of his land and cattle to drouth and to settle a note he had endorsed for a brother-in-law. He was on the verge of losing the rest in 1926 when a wildcat well came roaring in on his land. Drilled fifty miles from any proven production, this discovery opened the great Hendrick field, soon a veritable forest of the new-style steel derricks in contrast to the heavy wooden derricks so common at the time in other Basin fields.

George B. McCamey, Fort Worth drilling contractor, hit a double winner on September 27, 1925. His wife presented him a new son, and his test well – the first in Upton County – was confirmed as a solid producer. He gave his name to a new town.

There were many stories of forlorn hopes that paid off. Such a one was University No. 1-B, at 8,525 feet the deepest well in the world at the time it was drilled in 1928. Its drilling was plagued by misfortune, and when its costs ran past $100,000, a considerable amount for that day, its backers wanted to abandon what seemed a hopeless cause. Even the discouraged crew wanted to quit. Driller Cromwell, who had brought in Santa Rita No. 1, promised to close down but told his crew to "hit her another foot." That foot made the difference. Within a month the well was producing in excess of 1,600 barrels a day. More important, it encouraged even deeper drilling in the Basin.

Large ranch acreages were appreciated by landmen because they provided an opportunity to acquire significant blocks in one transaction. More troublesome were small holdings, which often required agreements with several landowners for putting together a suitable block for drilling. One refusal could nullify weeks of work and thousands of dollars in lease investments, making it impossible to complete a drilling project. Such a completion was a landman's nightmare. These frustrations were offset by successful negotiations like the one depicted in the Lovell painting of a midnight trade in a Basin farmhouse.

Development of a new oil field provided specialized work for large numbers of people: drilling crews, rig builders, roustabouts, teamsters. As production was firmly established, in came the tank builders and the pipeline construction companies. All the work was not in the fields. Much was supporting service in the canvas, raw-lumber and sheet-iron towns that sprang up almost in the shadows of the tall towers: rooming houses, hotels, garages, gas stations, grocery stores, theaters and dancehalls. Just behind these came schools for the workers' children.

Much has been said and written about the violence and sin of many early boomtowns, but often overlooked has been the fact that a great many of the people who followed oil development for the jobs and opportunity it offered had come from farms and small towns and were religious fundamentalists, steadfast in their faith. They conducted church services in the open or under tents and arbors until they found time and funds to put up a proper house of workship. Where the oilfielder went, the Bible went also.

The Basin's early development years created towns where there had been none at places like Crane, McCamey and Wink. It made cities out of such existing but quiet towns as San Angelo, Hobbs, Odessa and Midland. Midland, founded as a midway station house on the new Texas and Pacific Railroad in 1881, had long been a quiet and conservative ranching and farming town. Its central location amid the growing oil exploration and production made it a particular beneficiary. The region's first "skyscraper," Midland's million-dollar twelve-story Hogan Building, was at first derisively known as "Hogan's Folly," but it proved to be a most timely project, offering office space just when the oil companies so badly needed it. Other construction soon followed, and Midland's position as an industry center was secured.

Unlike many other oil-producing areas which boomed briefly and then withered to a shadow or even died, the Basin has remained productive and still supports exploration more than sixty years after the initial discovery wells were drilled. In an area long hard-put to furnish a livelihood for a relatively few hard-working farm and ranch people, the oil industry provided jobs and homes, hope and future for hundreds of thousands. It has had its cycles, up years and down years, fat years and lean. Despite this variability, it has produced wealth to help build a nation and energy to power the greatest country on earth, all this from a region which early observers dismissed as fit only for wild animals and desert nomads.

Tom Lovell's paintings vividly capture the spirit and the sweep of the Basin's colorful past.

Salt Bearers at Lake Juan Cordona   Oil on Canvas 30½ x 49"

SALT BEARERS AT LAKE JUAN CORDONA

For ages before white men learned of the new world, Indian dwellers of the Permian Basin and beyond traveled to the wind-swept salt bed that was to become known as Lake Juan Cordona, four miles north of the Pecos River in present Crane County. They brushed aside the thin top layer of blown-in sand and used sharp-pointed digging sticks to chip away at the caked salt beneath. The salt was a remnant of a receded ancient Pecos, its resting place reduced to a great T-shaped playa lake some two miles across, catching water only when rain came in abundance enough to run off from the greasewood-studded semi-desert that surrounded it.

How long ago primitive Indians first came to the lake for salt may never be known. Human bones discovered in the nearby Midland area have been estimated to be 10,000 to 15,000 years old. Spanish explorers found the migratory Jumanos on the banks of the Pecos, hunting buffalo afoot, gathering salt for trade.

Tom Lovell's painting depicts early Indians at lake's edge, a father and son carrying on their backs the yield of their labor in deerhide-lined wicker baskets supported by straps looped over their foreheads. Behind them, out on the shimmering surface of the crusted lakebed, others continue the eye-burning harvest. Lovell's Indians here are gatherers, not warriors, for they carry no weapons. They wear the yucca-fiber sandals of the desert dwellers in that primitive time before the horse, when the dog was their only domesticated animal, sometimes pet, sometimes beast of burden, sometimes supper.

Indians used salt to flavor and preserve meat, to cure animal hides and, sometimes, to draw game to places advantageous to the hunter. Salt was so vital that warring enemies sometimes maintained a truce at this lake and other salt sources of similar nature. It was a valuable item of trade. The farther the traders traveled from the salt deposits, the more meat, hides and farm products they could obtain in exchange.

The lake was reported by Antonio de Espejo in 1583. Spaniards, Mexicans and eventually Americans continued to dig salt from Lake Juan Cordona. What became known as the Old Salt Trail was developed from the Mexican town, Ojinaga, opposite Presidio on the Rio Grande. Though Horsehead was the most famous crossing on the Pecos, another known as the Salt Crossing was used near present Buena Vista in Pecos County.

Famous early cattleman Charles Goodnight told of his trip back down the Pecos after completion of his horrendous first cattle drive in 1866 upon what came to be known as the Goodnight-Loving Trail. On their way eastward toward the Conchos his party of cowboys saw what appeared to be a contingent of Indians coming toward them. All geared up for a fight, they found to their relief that the apparition was only an old settler named Rich Coffee, on his way to Lake Juan Cordona with a load of watermelons. He expected to sell them to Mexican salt gatherers and then load his wagon with salt for the return trip to his home near the junction of the Concho and Colorado Rivers east of later San Angelo.

Sacked salt from the lake was advertised in San Antonio newspapers in the 1870s. As late as the 1930s, stockmen in the region bought the sand-tinged salt for their sheep and cattle.

The lake gained its name from Juan Cordona, an early Texan of Mexican extraction who fought against Santa Anna in the Texas Revolution and was awarded the lake as part of a land grant from the Republic of Texas.

Today oilwells in and around the lakebed produce minerals of a kind undreamed-of by those who sharpened sticks and punched for salt along its dried edges during generations beyond counting.

Pecos Pueblo, about 1500   Oil on Canvas 35½" x 62½"

TRADING AT THE PECOS PUEBLO

*T*rading with neighboring tribes – and sometimes those from hundreds of miles away – was an ancient and honored custom among the Indians before the Europeans came. Barter enabled shells from the seacoast to find their way onto the high plains and water-carrying gourds grown in rich valley soils to find use in desert wickiups.

Tom Lovell has painted a scene at old Pecos Pueblo near the sundown of the Indian times, just before the coming of the first bearded ones out of Mexico was to begin the disintegration of an old civilization. Pecos Pueblo was some twenty-five miles east of Santa Fe, atop a low, flat mesa near the confluence of Glorieta Creek and the Pecos River just at the southern end of the Sangre de Cristo Mountains. It was settled about 1200 A.D. by Pueblo Indians and remained in constant use for more than six hundred years despite sometimes-savage intertribal warfare. Its steep approaches and its straight-up outer walls built of rock made it defendable against attack.

However, its position near the westernmost reaches of the open plains made it a strategic location for trading between the farming Indians of the valleys and the nomadic hunters who followed the buffalo and the rains and the grass. The painting depicts a peaceful trading scene between the permanently-settled Pueblos and a group of visiting Jicarilla Apaches, camped in buffalo-hide tepees at the foot of the *mesilla,* just beyond patches of standing corn. The camp is near enough for easy communication, yet far enough to present no serious threat to the five-storied stone settlement. An old Pueblo chief and two of his sons, standing, bargain with three Jicarilla chiefs whose people have brought buffalo robes, meat, tallow, flint and other goods to trade for corn, pumpkins, squash and similar products of the soil, as well as clay pottery artistically formed by the skilled and patient hands of the Pueblo women.

One of the kneeling Apaches holds across his knees a tobacco pouch and pipe which will be smoked to seal the bargain once the trading values have been established. The elderly Pueblo holds several turquoise necklaces to be used as gifts or trade items, along with the eagle in the willow cage, a symbol perhaps of the Indians' own imminent loss of freedom.

The cotton garments of the Pueblo Indians and the leather of the Jicarillas are indicative of their opposite lifestyles. Yet, an interdependence gives them a common meeting ground. The hunter needs the farmer, and the farmer needs the hunter.

The Jicarilla camp illustrates the importance of the dog as a bearer of Indian burdens in those long ages before the horse. *Travois* laden with robes and meat are lashed to the animals' backs. In moves between campsites, dogs dragged the lodgepoles and the skins to be erected as tepees. What the dogs did not drag, the women had to carry for long, weary miles and long, weary days while their menfolk guarded the column against attack by enemies.

Trading grounds such as these were usually regarded as sanctuary, temporarily immune from warfare so long as trading continued. This custom survived into white-man times when traders, trappers and Indians met annually at *rendezvous* to exchange furs, robes and trade goods. Blood enemies camped side by side and kept the truce until they left the trading grounds. Then it was open season again, and an enemy was an enemy wherever he might be encountered.

The artist notes that smoke from a few late breakfast fires drifts away toward the snow-topped Sangre de Cristos to become part of an overcast sky, foretelling the coming of the Spaniard and the end of an age-old way of life for the people of the prairies, the desert and the mountains.

Cabeza de Vaca   Oil on Canvas 33'' x 45''

CABEZA DE VACA

*N*o account of exploration and adventure surpasses that of the Spanish aristocrat and soldier Alvar Nuñez Cabeza de Vaca, whose westward wanderings took him from one Indian village to another across the Permian Basin in 1535, hardly more than forty years after Christopher Columbus first discovered the new world in his search for an old one. De Vaca came to the Americas to subdue Indians for his king but became a healer of Indians instead.

Descendant of illustrious fighters on both sides of his family, de Vaca was a lieutenant to the arrogant Panfilo de Narvaez, dispatched by King Charles V with some three hundred men in 1527 from Cuba to conquer Florida. The expedition was plagued by Narvaez' incompetence and decimated by murderous storms at sea. The disaster was compounded by determined Indian resistance, by exposure to merciless elements and by starvation. After a wretched series of incredible misfortunes, de Vaca and a handful of other survivors washed up on Galveston Island and fell into six years of dreadful hardship and attrition as slaves of the coastal Indians.

De Vaca and three others – Castillo, Dorantes and a Moorish slave known as Estevanico the Black – finally made a break for freedom in September 1534 when their captors trekked into the interior to gather fall-ripened prickly pear. The Spaniards traveled westward, enduring desperate hunger and thirst, hoping eventually to find "a land of the Christians."

In their long search across an unknown and sometimes barren land the bearded Spaniards were preceded from one Indian village to another by a reputation as faith healers, who had only to breathe upon the sick and bring them to full recovery. Wherever they went, they were beseeched to minister to the afflicted and dying. De Vaca himself was amazed at how often their prayers and feeble ministrations seemed to exert curative powers, and he began to believe that God had indeed endowed them with special blessings. His belief was buoyed by their own survival of terrible sufferings and dangers which had killed most of the rest of Narvaez' three hundred.

De Vaca's later account to the king indicates that the four visited the Conchos, watered at the present site of Big Spring, explored the Pecos River and saw the Davis Mountains, reaching the Rio Grande Valley below present El Paso. Always they were accompanied by large numbers of adoring Indians who cheerfully gave them all they had, though that was often precious little.

The Lovell painting depicts an occasion near the Pecos River. The Spaniards were brought an Indian suffering from an old war wound, a projectile point still lodged above his heart. After a prayer, de Vaca opened the man's chest with a flint knife, probing and cutting. Finding the object aslant, he worked it out with considerable difficulty, sewed up the wound with a bone needle and cartilage thread, then stanched the flow of blood with animal hair. The patient recovered. The arrowhead was passed among the marveling villagers and on into the back country to amaze those who had not witnessed the crude but effective surgery. Wrote de Vaca: "This cure so inflated our fame over the region that we could control whatever the inhabitants cherished."

Historians disagree about details of de Vaca's route, particularly its western part. Some say the travelers pushed through New Mexico and may have entered Arizona before bending southward into the Sonora Valley of Mexico, always seeking word of other Spaniards. At last, in March 1536, they met a party of slave-hunters under Captain Diego de Alcaraz. De Vaca's joy at reuniting with Christians after almost a decade of incredible misfortune was quickly tempered by dismay over their brutal treatment of the Indians. His long odyssey had given him a profound faith in God as a merciful father and a deep compassion for the Indians he had once sought to conquer.

De Vaca's efforts on the Indians' behalf created many enmities among the more venal of his countrymen and resulted in his being taken back to Spain in chains in 1543. A much-belated intercession by the king eventually freed him from years of abuse and allowed him to die with honor in 1557.

Coronado's Expedition Crossing the Llano Estacado   Oil on Canvas 35½ x 57½''

CORONADO'S EXPEDITION

*M*any of history's greatest accomplishments resulted from accident or error. So it was with the grand expedition of Don Francisco Vasquez de Coronado, commissioned by the viceroy of Mexico in 1540 to march northward and seek after the fabled gold, silver and emeralds supposed to exist in what would later become known as the American Southwest.

There seemed precedent enough for this belief that wealth abounded in that unknown land to the north of New Spain. Twenty years earlier, Cortez had sacked the Aztec empire, robbing that ancient civilization of shining treasures. Just four years before Coronado's huge column began its march, the long-lost Cabeza de Vaca had unexpectedly appeared in Mexico like a man resurrected from the dead, telling of riches seen or rumored during his long sojourn among the Indians of Texas.

Coronado started north from Compostela with an army consisting of 336 Spanish cavalry and infantrymen and several hundred Mexican Indians, accompanied by more than fifteen hundred horses and mules for riding and packing, as well as a large number of cattle, sheep and hogs to provide food along the line of march. By the time the column reached Texas it had already crossed Arizona and New Mexico. A scouting party had peered down from the rim across the awesome Grand Canyon of the Colorado. Coronado had crossed the continental divide and had visited the pueblos of the Zuni, Hopi and Tiguex. At Pecos Pueblo his men encountered a Plains Indian slave they called the Turk, who told of a rich land known as Quivira, far to the east. The Turk became Coronado's guide as he struck out across Texas in the spring of 1541.

Tom Lovell's painting finds the column on the Texas plains. The warm light of an early-morning sun shines upon armor and Toledo steel and reflects the expedition's anticipation as it advances toward the fabulous land of Quivira. The hope of riches is suggested by Coronado's armor, gilded to a golden sheen in contrast to the conventional gray and silver armor of his lieutenants. Though barely thirty at the time, Coronado rides with the stiff dignity of a much older commander, too much dignity perhaps to allow him the luxury of open laughter at whatever amusing story has just been told by his aide. At his right, two friars lead a mule bearing their holy oils and religious articles for the mass. A long pace ahead strides the Indian guide, carrying the dark secret of a personal mission. As far as the eye can see, soldiers and Indians, horses and the walking commissary of livestock string out in Coronado's dusty wake. Behind lie the blue-shadowed mesas and a land hitherto clouded in mystery, its secrets now laid open for exploitation by Europeans. Ahead lies a vast new land rich in grass and soil, a land one day to turn golden with wheat but yielding no gold of the kind Coronado seeks.

On the open plains of Kansas, a disillusioned Coronado will find that the sought-after golden city of Gran Quivira is but a thatched-hut village of the Wichita Indians. His long-building suspicions will lead him to torture the Turk into confessing that he has lured the expedition out upon the dry plains to see its provisions exhausted and its members perish under a hostile sun. An embittered Coronado will put the Turk to death, then begin a long and frustrating retreat, returning to Mexico in disgrace for failing to find something that was never there.

Regarded as a spectacular failure at the time, his exploration lifted a veil of darkness from the regions he traversed, opening the way to the conquest of the Southwest – for good or evil – by emissaries of Spain and by the many other Europeans who would follow the trail of Coronado.

Governor's Palace, Santa Fe, 1840   Oil on Canvas 36'' x 63''

GOVERNOR'S PALACE, SANTA FE

*T*hough Sante Fe lay well to the northwest of the Permian Basin, it influenced the history of the entire Southwest including the Basin during the time that old city was controlled by Spanish and Mexican governments. Santa Fe became a sought-after trade center for enterprising Yankee merchants who ofttimes observed the laws of Mexico only in the breach. Some early explorations of the Basin were undertaken by adventurers seeking obscure avenues of Mexican trade beyond the long reach of Sante Fe authorities.

Santa Fe was founded in 1610 as Spanish headquarters for the province of New Mexico under its first royal governor, Don Pedro de Peralta, who probably chose the site for its central location among the Indian pueblos as well as its accessibility from many diverse directions, its water and arable lands and the evident defensibility of the open ground. In the beginning it was serviced by infrequent caravans which required half a year to make the wearisome trip from Mexico City.

The seat of government was the Palace of the Governors, now considered the oldest public building, continuously used, within the continental borders of the United States. No construction date can be found, but this venerable structure must have been standing when the Pilgrims landed at distant Plymouth on a bleak and forbidding shore.

Tom Lovell's painting portrays a time of transition, of foreboding for the Mexican government which had ruled Santa Fe since Mexico won its independence from Spain in 1821. Now, in the bleak cold of early 1846, the Mexican War was building, and the shadow of the gringo lay long across the land. Here, at the corner of the palace already more than two centuries old, Mexican Governor Manuel Armijo stands in the snow at dusk and, by the flickering light of a lantern held by an aide, reads a dispatch just brought by horseback courier. The news was probably bad. Most of it was, by this twilight time of the Mexican reign.

Some old ways of life remained little changed since early Spanish times, as exemplified by the patient burro at far left, or the Indian's creaking oxcart carrying a load of hand-gathered firewood around the plaza. But after generations of relative isolation, the colonies of northern New Mexico had come under the strong influence of the *Americanos*. There had been the bold and raucous buckskinned mountain men who trapped the ice-fringed streams for beaver and frolicked away their earnings in the congenial atmosphere of Santa Fe and Taos. There had been the Yankee merchants who had brought their great Conestoga wagons across the Indian-dominated plains, the heavy iron rims cutting a track that would thereafter be known as the Santa Fe Trail. There had been filibusterers out of Texas and *Americano* soldiers like the pathfinder Zebulon Pike, encroaching on what had been virtually a closed society. They had imposed different values, aroused new tastes and new dreams among a simple people long regarded as tranquil and resistant to change.

Even beneath the stormclouds of approaching war, the Americans kept coming with their canvas-topped caravans, like the ox-drawn wagons moving along the edge of the plaza toward Armijo. The little military guard mount marching at the far right is symbolic of the weakness of Armijo's forces, the futility of their attempting a strong stand when the invasion comes.

At the end, Armijo would bow to reality. American President James K. Polk regarded New Mexico as a necessary stepping stone to the conquest of California, and he sent Stephen Watts Kearny westward with a 1,700-man army of conquest. Kearny's troops marched from Bent's Fort on the Arkansas River in Colorado and pushed through Raton Pass, guided by mountain men and traders who had already learned the secrets of this long-forbidden land. Armijo led his forlorn little force out to a natural fortress known as Apache Canyon, giving the appearance that he meant to defend the province. Suddenly he retreated to Santa Fe, paused only briefly, then fled to Albuquerque and finally to Chihuahua.

Kearny was amazed but delighted to meet no resistance. His army walked into Santa Fe unopposed on the afternoon of August 18, 1846, capturing the capital of New Mexico without firing a shot. The following day the remaining local authorities officially surrendered. The Mexican flag was hauled down from the palace, and the American flag went up.

Horsehead Crossing on the Pecos River   Oil on Canvas 30¾" x 59"

HORSEHEAD CROSSING OF THE PECOS RIVER

*T*ravelers who view the turgid Pecos River today in its sadly depleted and polluted state can hardly imagine the formidable obstacle it represented in earlier times before upstream dams and heavy invasion by water-wasting salt cedars choked off most of its flow. Relatively narrow, it was nevertheless deep and swift, too dangerous to cross except at a few points from the New Mexico line to its junction with the Rio Grande. Even they had their risks. Horsehead Crossing was the most famous of those fords.

Horsehead was used by Indians long before the first white travelers paused on its sloping banks after traversing the desert and contemplated the challenge of the rushing water that teased with its wetness and repulsed with its salt. Those first European travelers may well have been the Spaniard Cabeza de Vaca and his three companions.

For ages before they acquired the horse, Indians had used this ford in their migrations and in their salt-gathering trips to nearby Lake Juan Cordona. Once Indian foot soldiers became horseback warriors, able to ride hundreds of miles for grand raids into Mexico, they wore deep trails to this crossing point on the treacherous Pecos. Great herds of stolen horses and mules swam the river. Captive women and children were often divided here as raiding parties split up for the return to individual winter campsites. The raiders found captive children easier to handle when separated from their mothers, so this crossing became known among the Comanches as "the place of tears."

Horsehead was found by early traders taking their wagons toward Mexico, but its first heavy use by white men came during the Gold Rush to California in 1849.

Tom Lovell's painting depicts an 1850 crossing described by John R. Bartlett, mapping the region for the U.S.-Mexico Boundary Commission. Bartlett wrote: "Here there was a bank about half the height of the main bank, to which there was an easy descent, and one equally so to the water. I noticed a long line of horse or mule skulls placed along the bank, which probably gave it the name it bears."

His wagon was two-thirds across when the mules lost their footing and began to be swept away by the current. Mules were notoriously afraid of water. Oldtime teamsters said that when a mule got water in its ears it went into blind panic. Bartlett continued: "The last wagon, which had been behind, attempted to pass us...The current swept the wagon, which was half buried in water, against ours. This brought the mules nearly abreast of mine and lead to great confusion and alarm. Every moment we expected to be swept away, in which case our lives would have been in great danger."

When John Butterfield laid out his stageline in 1858, his coaches traveled from the head of the Middle Concho westward through Castle Gap and down the slope to Horsehead but did not cross over. Instead, they went up the east bank of the Pecos to Pope's Crossing just at the New Mexico line. The following year a ferry was built at Horsehead, and stages proceeded by the southern route to Comanche Springs, Fort Davis and El Paso. The line ceased operation upon the outbreak of the Civil War.

Horsehead became a crossing point for cattle herds after the war. Charles Goodnight and Oliver Loving started in June 1866 from Fort Belknap with two thousand head, their objective a new western route to Colorado. Following the old Butterfield Trail, they endured a hellishly hot and dry three days and nights and eighty miles without water from the head of the Conchos until their cattle smelled the Pecos and stampeded down to Horsehead. Some missed the ford and piled off the steep bank, one on top of another, drowning each other. Others bogged helplessly in quicksand. More than a hundred were lost, on top of three hundred left dead back along the dry trail. One of the bitterest experiences of Goodnight's life, it led the famous cattleman in later years to declare the Pecos River "the graveyard of the cowman's hopes."

Despite the hazards, many more herds followed the Goodnight-Loving Trail. Pitched battles were fought with Indians at and near Horsehead. Men were killed, horses and cattle lost to the red raiders. Until good roads and modern bridges caused its abandonment, Horsehead Crossing continued exacting a harsh toll upon those who used it.

Camels in Texas   Oil on Canvas 37'' x 57''

CAMELS IN TEXAS

*E*vil-smelling and evil-tempered, snorting, spitting and kicking at whatever displeased him, the gangling camel made an exotic but brief appearance as a Permian Basin pioneer. He fell from grace not for his shortcomings as a beast of burden but for the political and military misfortunes of the man responsible for bringing him here.

Secretary of War Jefferson Davis harbored a noble but doomed twenty-year dream that packtrains of water-thrifty camels could speed military supplies and commerce across inhospitable deserts of the West where horses, mules and oxen sometimes staggered and fell. In May 1856, thirty-three camels of varying origins offloaded from the naval storeship *Supply* at Old Powder Horn, a now-forgotten Texas port. With them came three Arab, Greek and Turk "camel-conductors" to handle the strange beasts and teach their craft to Americans. The Arab's name was Hadji Ali.

A caravansary was constructed at Camp Verde in the rugged Guadalupe River region between Bandera and Kerrville, duplicating those of the camels' homelands.

While these first dromedaries underwent heavy testing along challenging hill country trails, a second shipment of forty-one arrived in 1857.

The camels' nasty dispositions aroused the displeasure of soldiers and civilians alike. They panicked horses and mules into stampede at sight and scent and thereby caused the spilling of many a load and many a passenger. On one occasion, marauding Indians stole a pair of army camels. What they thought the creatures were and what they did with them, one can only imagine.

As Davis had hoped, the camels traveled long distances at a goodly clip while carrying loads far beyond the capacity of other pack animals. Lieutenant Edward F. Beale left for California in June, 1857, with a company of wagons, mules and camels, soon proving the humpies' able, if sometimes-reluctant, performance on the *Great American Desert*.

Tom Lovell's painting depicts an incident in June 1859, when Lieutenant William H. Echols commanded a party of 25 camels and 25 mules, accompanied by U.S. Infantry and Arab drivers, on a trip of exploration from Camp Hudson on the Devils River northwest of present Del Rio, across the Trans-Pecos to Fort Davis, then south to Presidio del Norte, the Big Bend and back to Camp Hudson, testing the animals against the most brutal of terrain.

Initially the beasts were roped together on the trail. In this scene, based on an actual happening, one of the camels working its way up a sloping bare rock lost its footing and fell, smashing a water barrel in a thirsty land where water was precious almost beyond measure. One of Echols' officers quickly cut the line and prevented a bad situation from becoming worse.

The painting depicts one camel climbing a rock bench on its knees, a characteristic which gave it an edge over horses and mules. A male camel on this trip was packed with five hundred pounds, a female three hundred. They endured four hot days without water, something horses and mules could not do.

By this time, however, Jefferson Davis' attention was being diverted to a problem of much graver import than his camels, the imminent secession of the Southern states and the outbreak of a war in which he would cast his lot against the federal government he had so long and diligently served.

In February 1861, Camp Verde passed into Confederate hands with eighty camels and two Egyptian drivers. As one oldtimer later said, the Confederates did not know what use to make of the camels. "They were like a wart on a stick. We had them and couldn't get rid of them." Some were put to work packing cotton to the Mexican border. Camels became so unpopular that Brownsville on the Rio Grande enacted an ordinance against them.

When the cannons at last went silent and the Union reoccupied Camp Verde, just forty-four camels remained. In the leftover hatreds of war, anything associated with Jefferson Davis, president of the failed Confederacy, became anathema. The federals sold their remaining camels. Some went into circuses. Others packed freight in the far West, straying and scattering, turning up unexpectedly in the desert for years afterward like some unworldly apparition, frightening the unwary and reminding others about a page of history almost forgotten.

The Arab Hadji Ali lived out a long life in the desert West under the nickname Hi-Jolly and became a figure in Arizona legend.

Captain Pope's Well   Oil on Canvas 38½'' x 65½''

CAPTAIN POPE'S WELL

*C*aptain John Pope has been called "America's first Wildcatter." Unlike latter wildcatters in the Permian Basin, however, his search was not for oil. He sought artesian water for an envisioned transcontinental railroad. A Kentuckian and West Pointer, brevetted captain after Monterrey and Buena Vista in the Mexican War, this army engineer surveyed a prospective railroad route across Texas in 1854. He found one major obstacle: lack of water. He proposed the drilling of four water wells at twenty-five mile intervals between the Pecos and the Colorado.

Given a Congressional appropriation of $100,000, he set up camp east of the Pecos River in present Loving County, seven miles below the 32nd Parallel. He began drilling in June, 1855, near the mouth of Delaware Creek. His first well portended the trouble and frustration that would plague his project for three years. Water at 360 feet caved off the side of the hole and forced him to put down casing. He ran out of tubing at 500 feet. More water at 600 feet collapsed the bottom part and forced abandonment. Pope tried a second site near Las Cruces,

New Mexico, but struck rock at 293 feet after three-and-a-half months.

A third attempt began in April, 1856, five miles east of the ill-fated first hole and just north of the Texas-New Mexico line. At 450 feet a piece of tube near the bottom gave way. As much tubing as possible was withdrawn from the hole, and a fresh start began May 20. By July the supply of wooden drilling rods was used up in 809 feet of clays, marls and soft sandstone. Pope converted ash-wood tent poles to the purpose, but they were quickly chewed in two. At 861 feet, he had to go to Washington for more money. Despite his difficulties, he remained convinced that artesian water existed, just a little deeper. He returned to the Pecos with a crew of experienced drillers and better equipment: a steam boiler, engine and pump to re-enter the well.

Tom Lovell's painting depicts this discouraging final phase in the bitter winter of 1857-58. Captain Pope, on horseback at one leg of the forty-foot tripod derrick, talks to a civilian geologist and a blacksmith while a dragoon lieutenant listens. The crew prepares for bailing by pulling drilling rods out of the hole and unscrewing their sixteen-foot threaded sections, laying them neatly on the ground. At the portable steam engine, a tender stokes the ever-hungry, wood-burning boiler.

A six-mule Army wagon hauls in supplies, and an open wagon stands with a freshly-gathered load of mesquite roots to add to the fuel pile beside the boiler's water barrels. Crude picket corrals at far left confine the few horses and mules not sent to Fort Davis for better feed and more adequate protection from the cold, wet weather which has made winter miserable for the civilian crew and military stationed at this bleak and windswept site. At far right, dragoons prepare to patrol for Indian sign. Contemporary records offer no evidence that Indians ever bothered Pope's camp in the three years he spent drilling in hostile country, though they probably observed from afar and wondered at the steaming, clanking monster beneath what must have appeared to them to be three huge tepee poles.

Pope had problems enough; he did not need Indians. Despite the most efficient equipment then available, and a skilled crew, he reported the project beset by "repeated accidents and breakages of machinery." The alkaline Pecos River water mercilessly eroded the boiler and clogged it with scale. The crumbly sides of the hole kept caving in until they made it impossible to force the casing deeper and protect the bottom. Rock grated away the wooden drilling rods and bent those of iron. At 1,053 feet, remarkable for that time, the well was finally abandoned. Four years of planning and hard work were pronounced a failure.

But failure or not, Pope had pioneered deep drilling in the Permian Basin. His experiences aided those who came after him, seeking oil rather than water.

Several ironies awaited the enterprising captain. As his troops left the abandoned project, scouts found shallow water in the Monahans sands to the east. Because of the Civil War, it would be thirty years before a railroad finally laid tracks along the route he had surveyed. In that war, Pope distinguished himself under Ulysses S. Grant at the Battle of Vicksburg. But then, risen to major general, he lost the second Battle of Manassas, or Bull Run. For the duration of his military career he was relegated to minor assignments. His battleground failure blighted the remainder of his life.

He did not live to see his drilling work honored by later generations which ventured deeper and brought up oil.

Comanche Moon   Oil on Canvas 35½" x 63"

COMANCHE MOON

By the time white men began to visit the Permian Basin in significant numbers, the dominant Indian tribe was the warlike Comanche, long the most formidable barrier to permanent settlement. But dominance had not always been the Comanches' lot. They were, in fact, a splendid example of turnabout, of the underdog winning his day.

The Comanches were an estranged branch of the Shoshones, for ages restricted to eking out a marginal subsistence on poor lands along the western edge of the Rockies. They were much put-upon by more powerful neighboring tribes, a condition for which they extracted abundant revenge once they came into possession of the Spanish horse by trade or theft. They quickly mastered the use of this strange new beast for hunting and warfare. Within a generation the speed and mobility of the horse transformed them from one of the most vulnerable of the plains peoples to one of the most feared. They migrated southward, wresting choice hunting grounds from other tribes until they had taken primary possession of a huge buffalo range from the Arkansas River in southern Colorado all the way to the hill country west of San Antonio, including most of the Permian Basin.

Intensely proud and quick to fight, they were a loose confederation of distantly related bands who called themselves "the people," implying that they were the chosen and all others were lesser beings. They made alliances of convenience with certain other tribes, particularly the Kiowas, but never regarded them as equals.

Each fall before settling into winter encampments, Comanches from the high plains struck southward upon a grand raid. Their pathway became known as the Comanche War Trail, so hoof-worn that much of it was still visible a generation after the raids ceased. It crossed the Permian Basin and the Big Bend, extending well into the interior of Mexico. A lone Comanche warrior once created panic in the streets of Chihuahua City. One raiding party penetrated so far into the Mexican jungles that it encountered chattering monkeys and brightly-plumed parrots, to the warriors' great amazement. This annual raiding time became dreaded as the Comanche Moon, not only in Mexico but in Anglo settlements along the western frontier of Texas.

Tom Lovell's painting depicts the triumphant return of a Comanche-Kiowa raiding party to its village beside Comanche Springs, at present Fort Stockton. It was customary for the warriors to stop short of camp after a successful raid, painting and decorating themselves and their horses for a grand entry while some low-ranked member of the party rode ahead and alerted the village to prepare for their imminent return.

The most honored warriors head the procession, displaying scalps they have taken. The leader wears a buffalo-horn headdress and boastfully waves a lance displaying three new scalps, a fourth tied to his horse's lower lip. He carries a bull-hide shield decorated with symbols of his individual *medicine*. Around his neck dangles a war whistle made of an eagle's legbone. Behind him, astride a small mule, a frightened young Spanish captive girl is already the object of abuse by two squaws who have moved up to strike at her. She will probably be turned over to the women for the meanest of slave labor until she is ready to become a bride and bear a warrior's children. Beside her rides a captive boy, who may remain a slave so long as he survives or may, if fortunate, be accepted eventually for training as a warrior and become, in effect, a Comanche himself.

A few men carry trophy muskets and powderhorns, but most still rely on the bow, in their hands often a more dangerous weapon than any firearm. Bringing up the rear of the procession are horses taken as booty, to be divided among the warriors according to their rank and contribution to the raid. Some may become gifts to favored elders or be traded for wives. The Comanche counted his wealth in horses.

Had the raid been unsuccessful and heavy casualties taken, this joyous scene would not have occurred. The warriors would have stolen into camp under cover of darkness, and the lodges of the fallen would resound with the wailing of their women. Any captives who had survived that far would probably have been slaughtered for vengeance.

Fast Mail to Carlsbad   Oil on Canvas 36½'' x 50½''

FAST MAIL TO CARLSBAD

In the first years that the automobile appeared in the Permian Basin, there was good cause to ask whether it was really an improvement over the horse. It was faster, of course, when it was moving, but often it was stalled with a flat tire or a boiled-dry radiator, or so deeply mired in a mudhole that only a stout team of horses or mules offered salvation. And even the cheapest plug horse knew better than to run blindly into a ditch. But improvement came swiftly, and by 1910 it was apparent that horses under a steel hood would win out over horses in leather harness.

A new open-topped 1910-model Maxwell automobile went into service carrying mail on the long road from Midland to Carlsbad, a task previously performed by horse-drawn vehicles. It was a two-day trip in each direction, with an overnight stop in Seminole. Slow as that might seem, it was faster than a wagon or buckboard. Freighters would leave Midland at daylight, bound for Seminole or Lamesa, and camp their wagons the first night about twenty miles out. The Maxwell made that leg of its journey in a little more than two hours if it did not encounter unusual difficulties.

Tom Lovell's painting depicts a stop for radiator water at a windmill between Midland and Seminole, possibly on the Chicago Ranch. The driver augmented income from the mail route by carrying passengers. Male passengers could not count on being along simply for the ride, however. They could expect to help with tire changes, water-carrying or other necessary chores that might arise. Such is the case here. While two women passengers gather wildflowers from the prairie, the driver checks a tire and the men passengers fetch water in canvas bags to fill the radiator. When the heavily-laden automobile leaves, those bags will have been filled again in case more water is needed short of the next windmill.

Such a trip in early motoring times required planning and preparation. A driver had to be something of a mechanic. He carried a full set of tools to meet an emergency that might befall him on the road. He was likely to have more than one extra tire in case he suffered a puncture or blowout too big to patch. Automobiles were still a comparative rarity except in town, so it was possible he might not meet another in a full day's journey. At best he was likely to meet a few wagons or buggies, or cowboys on horseback. Some days he might not meet anyone. He had to depend upon himself and what he carried.

The road he traveled was a wagon track, worn into twin-rut permanence, meandering around hills and mottes of brush, usually zigzagging from one windmill to another out of respect for the horse and mule teams which needed water every few miles. At each fence was a gate to be opened, often a difficult wire gate with an old jaw-buster horsecollar-hame latch that could inflict grievous pain upon the unwary. A driver on unfamiliar and unmarked roads might find himself dead-ended at a windmill or a cowcamp miles from the point where he went wrong.

The windmill is an Eclipse type with wooden tower and cypress fan, popular with ranch and farm people of that time and typical not only of the Permian Basin but of the entire Southwest. The mills' principal shortcoming was the absolute necessity of greasing them every few days, not only a dirty job but also a dangerous one when the wind was high. Most large ranches had windmill men whose only assignment was to keep the wheels turning and the water pumping. Easier-maintained steel fans supplemented most of the Eclipses by the 1930s.

Familiarity with the drilling of water wells and the handling of windmill casings and suckerrods would help many ranch workers move easily into the oilfield labor force when petroleum development came to the Basin.

An irony for the wagon freighters who traveled the same road as this Maxwell was that an increasingly important cargo item for them was barrels of gasoline to power the growing numbers of automobiles and trucks that soon would drive the wagon-and-team operators out of business and into history.

Though the scattering of people living in the Basin had no inkling of it at the time, the need to fuel the combustion engine was destined soon to transform their region and merge its destiny with that of a new and vibrant industry.

Free Lunch on the Slaughter Ranch   Oil on Canvas 34¾″ x 56¾″

FREE LUNCH ON THE SLAUGHTER RANCH

*I*n the wake of the military and the final retreat of the Indians who so long had claimed the land, life in the Permian Basin became geared to the expansion of the ranching industry. Its pace was that of the horse, an easy walk most of the time, picking up to a short gallop on occasion. The wildcatter Carl Cromwell, using an inexperienced crew of cowboys in Reagan County, drilled a well dubbed Santa Rita, after the Patron Saint of the Impossible. Life's pace in the Basin was never to be the same after that morning of May 28, 1923, when oil suddenly went over the top of Cromwell's wooden derrick.

The Santa Rita was not actually the Basin's first oilwell. Production had been established in Mitchell County, but it was not on the scale that would be developed as a result of the Reagan County discovery. The Santa Rita well, and those which followed it, meant financial salvation to many landowners, hard-pressed by drouth and the ups and downs of cattle and sheep prices. Stories are legion in the Basin's folklore about ranchmen and farmers pulled back from the brink of foreclosure by the timely arrival of a landman or a cabletool rig and crew.

Oil was not an unmixed blessing. It brought an invasion of geologists and drillers, of speculators and fortune hunters, of builders and boomers. New roads spiderwebbed the grazing lands, and mule teams bladed off oilwell locations at a heavy cost in grass. When a well came in, acres around it were often blackened and ruined. Water was sometimes spoiled. Cattle drank from the slush pits and were poisoned, or wandered out into them and drowned. Gates were left open and fences knocked down. Ranching could be difficult in an oilfield.

But most landowners adjudged the potential income worth the cost. Seeing the financial benefit to friends and neighbors, many actively sought the oil men's favorable attention. Among them was J. A. Slaughter, featured in Tom Lovell's painting. Slaughter operated the large and historic U Lazy S Ranch, pioneered by John B. Slaughter near Post in Garza County. In 1924 he invited a group of geologists to his ranch to enjoy a chuckwagon dinner, hoping they might find inspiration to explore the drilling possibilities.

The painting depicts a hypothetical gathering of men prominent in the development of Permian Basin oil and gas production. From the left, clockwise, they include Berte R. Haigh, geologist, looking through a then-new surveying instrument known as an alidade; Robert W. "Bob" Patteson, oil scout; O. C. "Kip" Harper, geologist; J. A. Slaughter, the ranch owner; Charles D. Vertrees, geologist, the man hunkered down near the chuckwagon, a coffee cup in his hand; Stanley Jay, geologist, the bareheaded man sitting on a cowboy's tied bedroll at right; and D. E. "Cap" Lounsbery, geologist, sitting on the spread-out tarp-covered bed.

These were the advance men essential to the exploration and expansion of the oil industry in West Texas and New Mexico. On their judgment rested the investment or the withholding of millions of dollars in land leases and drilling funds. It was little wonder that a rancher's heart might lift with joy at a favorable nod from a geologist who found a promising surface contour beneath meandering cow trails.

The scene illustrates the combination of the traditional and the new in the transitional 1920s. The chuckwagon, credited to the creative imagination of early Texas cattleman Charles Goodnight, had been the mobile outdoor kitchen for cow outfits since shortly after the Civil War.

Horse or mule teams remained its motive power. The water barrel was still a necessity when the wagon camped away from streams of windmills in a country where water was scarce. The whitefaced Hereford cattle in the background had largely supplanted the original Longhorns by about the turn of the century, but the manner of working them was still little changed in the 1920s except for the convenience of pasture fences to limit the animals' wanderings and confine the scale of the roundup.

A touch of modern times is the windup clock which awakens the cook at perhaps four in the morning to fix breakfast so well-fed cowboys can be ready to ride by first light. Even newer is the battery-powered radio with morning-glory speaker, bringing the news of the world and music from distant city studios to compete with the bawling of cattle and the howling of coyotes on the open prairie.

Plane Table Party on King Mountain   Oil on Canvas 27'' x 42''

PLANE TABLE PARTY NORTHEAST
OF McCAMEY

For decades after the Permian Basin became known by the white man, relatively few made their homes in it. To most, it was an inhospitable country where the flora and fauna were armed for protection by horns and fangs, thorns and barbs, where grass was sparce and water was salty or flavored with gyp, and always in short supply. It was a region to be crossed as hurriedly as possible on the way to more congenial environs. It was the last part of Texas to settle up.

Even into the early 1920s its inhabitants were mostly ranchers and the people of small railroad towns and county seats that served the ranches. Farming maintained a foothold where soil was good and deep, irrigated from the few rivers and streams. Away from the watered lands, dryland farmers bet their hopes and their labor against the hot, dry summers. They lost, more often than not.

Then came oil, and those long-shunned lands were suddenly sought after, poked over, explored as never before for the wealth hidden beneath that formidable surface. Across lands once known only to the Indian and in more recent times the cowboy, geologists drove primitive automobiles long and punishing miles through greasewood and mesquite, prickly pear and *lechuguilla*. When steel and rubber could go no farther, they walked in protective high-laced boots, searching for surface signs that might mean oil.

As warriors in an earlier time had climbed to the high places to seek out their spirits and gain insight into their destinies, these questing oil men climbed the mountains and the mesas to study the far reaches of open ground below. From those vantage points they could see rises and depressions that might indicate how a restless earth in ages past had twisted and contorted and buckled, trapping oil in formations thousands of feet beneath.

Tom Lovell depicts geologist D. E. "Cap" Lounsbery

and George T. Abell, then representing Midwest Refining Company, working with a plane table on top of King Mountain northeast of McCamey. They are but the latest participants in a long cavalcade of history which has marched across this land. Not far distant lies Castle Gap, a point of passage for travelers since ancient times. Indians had long traversed the plain near the point where the geologists have left their automobile far down at the foot of the mountain. Forty-niners on their way to California had left wagon tracks there, to be followed by stagecoaches of the Butterfield line. Down there the tortured cattle herd of Goodnight and Loving had plodded its final miles in desperate thirst before scenting the waters of the Pecos and stampeding wildly to Horsehead Crossing.

Down there somewhere the fabled treasure of Maximilian was supposedly buried by men who never lived to recover it. But these geologists seek a greater treasure, one that would provide employment to thousands, build towns where there had been prairie and cities where there had been towns.

The plane table and an alidade were used to chart the contours of the surface, mapping the topography for analysis of the geologic structures that might lie beneath. Plane-table mapping was customarily done by a two-man team. At least one would be a geologist who selected the area to be mapped, carrying with him a sixteen-foot stadia rod and recording the geologic information. The instrument man remained at the plane table, aligning the cross hairs of his alidade with markings on the stadia rod held by the geologist. He determined the direction and distance of each location and, by noting the vertical angle of the telescope, calculated the elevation. This survey effort produced a three-dimensional map that betrayed contours not always visible to the eye.

This type of field work was exacting and tough, confined largely to young men who had the stamina to walk long miles over rough country beyond the reach of their automobiles, to tolerate heat and cold, hunger and thirst, bad food and gyppy water. Their life was at times but little more comfortable than that of the pioneers who had crossed this land before them.

Bride's Home at a Wildcat Well   Oil on Canvas 21½'' x 36½''

A BRIDE'S HOME AT A WILDCAT WELL

*L*ike pioneer women for generations before them, wives of the early oil men followed their husbands into sometimes desolate environments, yet managed somehow to make a home. Tom Lovell's painting celebrates the resilient spirit of these women who carried civilization with them wherever they went and planted its seed even in the most barren of soil.

This is a wildcat driller's camp, the tall wooden derrick of a cabletool rig standing tall against a blue sky that has managed sometime in the recent past to provide at least a little spring rain and carpet the ground with bright yellow wildflowers amid the cactus and greasewood and low-growing mesquite. The young bride has finished her morning wash and hung it on a makeshift line to dry in the desert wind. While the fire slowly dies beneath the blackened washpot, she has walked out into her vast open "yard" with tin plate in hand to feed her flock of "chickens," a covey of blue quail. Her husband has finished his work shift and sits resting on the steps of their new pine-board and tarpaper shack, admiring the pretty girl who has chosen to share with him both the

hardships and the simple pleasures of a life miles from town or railroad, miles from electricity or running water, miles even from another woman who might help ease the loneliness of her long days.

Lonely or not, it is an adventure, the kind for which youth seems to have been invented. It is a shared adventure to re-live in memory for the rest of her life, though she might never want to do it over again. This once it is fresh and new, brightened by discovery, faith and hope that outweigh the hardships. In later years, looking back from a time of relative comfort that this experience will help provide, she will know the hardships for what they were, and she will probably not regret a one.

Life had a rough and primitive edge in those early-day drilling camps and in the oil boomtowns they brought into being. The Permian Basin was big, awesomely so, the miles long and difficult. For each newcomer there was, for one thing, a disconcerting feeling of isolation from distant homes and from family left behind.

Even in a house such as the one in the painting, the outdoors was always coming inside. Summer heat was a living thing that trapped itself within the walls and could not seem to get out. Winter winds whistled through the siding and up under the floor, overwhelming the best efforts of a wood-burning stove. Rolldown canvas curtains outside the windows never managed to turn back the dust and the gritty sand that forever sought entry and filtered down into the food, into the beds, even into boxes and trunks that held the good clothes and the treasured keepsakes from back home.

Of dust and sand there was always more than enough. It was a more fragile land than its formidable appearance might suggest, its vegetation thin and easily disturbed by the constant traffic always a part of oilfield development. Rain was infrequent, so that the vegetation was slow to re-establish itself, if it ever did. The bared soil was easily stirred by whatever moved, or by the wind that searched ceaselessly across the Basin.

Water was scarce. Though drillers often punched through water strata in their search for the deeper oil, well locations typically had no water of their own. Every drop used had to be hauled in by wagon or truck. In boomtowns like McCamey and Crane, residents bought their water by the barrel at high price and stretched it as far as they could.

Unsure when they might have to move to another field, another town, families might live in tents or small "shotgun" shacks, even occasionally in converted buses that foreshadowed the mobile homes of a later generation. It was not unusual in Permian Basin boomtowns to see a fine new automobile, symbol of steady work and good wages, parked in front of a boarded-up tent, symbol of the impermanence of these quickly-sprouted, quickly-wilted oases in the desert.

It was a young industry, and these were young people, for the most part. They were pioneers of a new kind, yet they were close kin in spirit to all those earlier pioneers who had passed this way. And where the pioneer woman went, home went also.

A Trade at Midnight   Oil on Canvas 35½'' x 45½''

A TRADE AT MIDNIGHT

Before a driller could spud in at a new location, even before the loan could be obtained to send the driller and his rig *to* that location, the landman had to complete his work. It was his responsibility to negotiate with owners of the mineral rights for authority to explore for oil and gas. And though he was trying to buy rather than sell, he had to be a salesman, persuading the holders of those rights that his was a fair offer, better than anyone else was likely to give.

The scene Tom Lovell has painted was played out countless times in the early days of Permian Basin oil exploration. It continues in developing areas today, the landman offering, the owners considering risks and benefits, wondering if it might pay to hold out for more.

The artist based this scene on an actual event described to him by George T. Abell, an independent operator prominent in the Basin's development. The hour is late in a small and simple but clean and pleasant farmhouse. The minute hand moves toward midnight on the old-fashioned clock shelved high up the kitchen wall. The old black range has long since gone cold. The landman had come about dark after a long, challenging day of negotiating oil and gas leases with the farmer's neighbors in a desperate effort to put together a block large enough to justify drilling a test well in an unproven area. He had arrived tired and hungry, but he could not afford to rest until he was through.

Though his coat and tie hint of prosperity and contrast with the farmer's blue work shirt, the truth is that several dry holes have brought him almost to the end of his rope. Unless he can make this deal and fit this parcel of land into the block he has been trying to put together, he cannot obtain financial backing to go ahead with the well his instinct and the geologists' reports tell him will turn his luck around. Without this lease, he may be finished as an independent oil man.

The farmer's financial situation is equally precarious. He has endured several drouthy years, and his debts at the bank have built to a critical point. He needs the money from the oil lease to pay his grocery bill and continue feeding his family. His land taxes have gone unpaid and threaten his ability to hold the farm. It is essential to his and his family's survival on this land that he obtain the best possible deal on the lease.

So, despite the fact that he and his wife are both weary from a hard day's work in the field, he has sparred for hours with the landman. Whatever he does will be a gamble. If the well comes in dry, he may never be offered another lease. In such a case, what he receives now may be all he ever gets; he cannot afford to lease too cheaply. Again, if he leases for too little and a good well is made, the lease is locked in, and he will have nothing left to sell in the future except the royalty. He wants to preserve that for his family. If he holds out for too much, he fears the bidder may tire of the struggle and leave, for it is natural that the landman has not divulged the extent of his own need.

Now, near midnight, the futures of the farm family and of the oil man hang in the balance. A decision must be made. The little girl, shoes off, has gone to sleep with her head in her mother's lap. The boy, older, has tried to show his maturity by staying awake and keeping up with the bargaining that he realizes affects his own welfare, but now he dozes, pillowing his head upon his arm on the little kitchen table. The dog faithfully hangs on, but he too would rather lie down and go to sleep.

The landman knows his financial limitations, and he has stretched them in the long evening of negotiation. But now, before giving up, he adds one extra sweetener to the offer and again unfolds the contract in the light of the kerosene lamp. "To boot," he says, "I'll pay your taxes up to date."

That makes the crucial difference, for the taxes have weighed heavily on the farmer's mind. He glances at his wife and sees her smile. He looks up at the landman and senses that this is as far as he can go. Besides, the offer is fair. The farmer arises from the table and extends his hand. "It's a deal," he declares.

The story as told to the artist had a happy ending for all participants. The well was good, affording years of royalty payments to farmers who signed the leases. The landman went on to a long career as a successful independent producer.

THE PERMIAN BASIN PETROLEUM MUSEUM

As we drive along Interstate 20 in south Midland and our gaze wanders to a horizon that appears as a flat line against a blue West Texas sky, we are drawn to the unexpected sight of a tall wooden derrick over half a century out of its time. It seems incongruous against a distant cluster of modern steel and glass skyscrapers rising out of the prairie, marking downtown Midland's nerve center for today's still-bustling oil industry.

The derrick beckons us to the Permian Basin Petroleum Museum, largest of its kind in the nation. Beneath that sturdy wooden frame, the walking beam of old Santa Rita No. 2 still labors in stolid see-saw fashion as it has since 1923. That year the Reagan County well over which it stood was drilled as a sister to fabulous Santa Rita No. 1, the wildcat discovery that touched off the Permian Basin's biggest boom. The lone tower reminds us that once such derricks stood in veritable forests, pumping lifeblood for a mechanized nation.

Turning off the interstate and onto an access road that brings us to the Museum entrance, we find ourselves driving toward three working pumpjacks of the type that commonly occur across the world in today's oil fields. They stand there in three sizes like Papa Bear, Mama Bear and Baby Bear. They are an American, a Lufkin and a tiny Jensen, a multiple completion arrangement designed to draw oil from three different depths, each a separate pay zone.

We park and walk first for a closer look at the rig which initially caught our attention, old Santa Rita No. 2, moved eighty miles from Texon to the Museum site in 1974. Much of this cable tool rig, except the rebuilt derrick portion, is still original. The first wooden derrick stood over No. 2's well until it was replaced in 1938 by one of steel. By the time the rig was moved to the Museum almost forty years later, the metal structure was badly deteriorated. A decision was made to reconstruct a

The Old and the New   by Permission of Jesus Mercado

replica of the original wooden derrick, eighty-three feet tall. Veteran rig builder, Q. L. "Shorty" Hall of Odessa oversaw the project in the accepted manner of the 1920's, by "eyeball," without drawings. No. 2 is believed to be the oldest such cable tool rig still surviving in the Basin, one of fewer than ten of its vintage anywhere in the Southwest and fewer than twenty-five in the entire United States.

Standing on the west side opposite Santa Rita No. 2 and a modern heater-treater is National No. 3, a portable drilling machine which saved drillers the cost of building derricks. All-steel, it was designed to penetrate as deeply as 3,500 feet. It was used in the 1950s and was still operational when it became part of the Museum's permanent outdoor exhibit.

Not far from No. 2 stands a "Christmas Tree" of the type used to control pressure and govern the flow of a well into a pipeline. Its collection of valves and wheels led to its nickname among oil field workers.

Centered in a landscaped and grassed oasis waits a simple yet handsome museum structure of some 45,000 square feet, seemingly dwarfed by the broad and open West Texas skyline but much larger than its single-story elevation makes it appear. It is positioned toward the front of a forty-one acre pasture still left for the most part to nature, to the low-growing mesquite and prickly pear, the spear-pointed yucca, the tumbleweed, to the jackrabbit, dove and quail, the burrowing owl and the ground squirrel, to the rattlesnake and the roadrunner.

Museum Portico   Courtesy, Roland K. Smith

This building is oil man George T. Abell's dream. He wanted no dead, dusty shelves stacked full with dead, rusty equipment. He wanted a vibrant, living museum that would speak with the voices of the men who built the oil industry and that would ring with the clamor and the noise of the tools they used to bring energy up from the depths of the earth.

The Museum has reflected his dream. More than forty-five thousand people have filed through each year since it opened in 1975. Among them have been some eight thousand children on annual school field trips, children who respond eagerly to living exhibits that invite them to touch and experience, that surprise them and fire their imaginations.

As we enter the outer tall glass doors we pass through the wide lobby, pausing at the book and gift counter. Beyond a second set of doors we encounter the living map, a talking display of changing pictures and maps which summarize what the Museum is about, the beginnings of oil and gas in early geologic time, the beginning, the present and the future of the petroleum industry.

For a historical perspective that lends to a more rounded understanding of the modern generation's role in the Permian Basin, we browse first along and between

West Wing Entrance   Courtesy, Roland K. Smith

the gently curving walls of the west wing. Here we find reflected the broad panorama of human experience in the Permian Basin during the final long centuries before oil and gas were discovered. Maps and artifacts such as arrow points, pottery, blankets and leather moccasins are supplemented by photographs and fine paintings. The latter, by the respected Tom Lovell, represent the tenacious prehistoric Indians who inhabited this drouth-prone region, managing to survive and build a culture despite the sparcity of vegetation and game, the long distances between watering places.

Paintings depict the coming of Europeans, led by the shipwrecked Spaniard Cabeza de Vaca, wandering afoot across the forbidding Pecos River region, healing worshipful Indians while he searched for people of his own kind. They present Coronado and those who followed, claiming the region first for Spain, later for Mexico, and finally — with the coming of the Americans — for the United States. They tell of early military explorations, of the ambitious but ill-fated camel experiment, of Captain John Pope's first wildcat drilling ventures, seeking water rather than oil. An array of ancient rifles reflects not only the evolution of firearms but their vital role in the exploration and settlement of the Southwest.

A section features the history of ranching in the Permian Basin, the principal economic activity before oil exploration brought a new way of life. Cattle brands, once called the heraldry of the range, are represented by a selection of branding irons from many of the area's better-known ranches. We are invited to turn by hand an Axtell windmill fan, twelve feet in diameter, reminding us that several generations of Basin dwellers had been drilling into the earth before the first oil man came. Like Captain Pope, however, they were searching for water, not for petroleum.

The last Lovell paintings, along with several by the gifted John Scott and Frank Gervasi, depict for us the Basin's pioneering oil ventures, the everyday working life of men at wildcat rigs, in the oil fields and the early boomtowns. Old photos, much enlarged so we may enjoy their detail, show the look of such Basin towns as Crane, Goldsmith, Hobbs, Iraan, McCamey, Midland, Odessa, Texon and Wink at the peak of their early booms. We examine a genuine old buckboard used on the rough roads and rougher ribbon-marked traces of the West Texas oil fields. We find it still has its built-on racks that carried fishing tools for recovery of objects lost deep in a well. Nearby we see an alidade of the type used in mapping surface contours for manifestations of underground structures where oil might be found. We study O. C. "Kip" Harper's original 1924 Permian Basin geological map, regarded by many as one of the most significant pieces of geological evaluation ever done in the United

States, for it demonstrated the existence of the Central Basin Platform and was pivotal in latter explorations.

One section of the west wing is set aside for special limited-time exhibits. These change periodically to offer the repeat visitor something new along with a reinspection of the more familiar.

Our tribute to history continues in the Petroleum Hall of Fame Room, where we find portraits of sixty-four men whose contributions lent significantly to development of the petroleum industry in the Permian Basin and elsewhere. The portraits hang on either side of a two hundred-pound centerpiece constructed, appropriately enough, of acrylic, a petroleum by-product. New inductees are limited to no more than four every two years. Though most are or were oil men, several made contributions of an indirect nature, including an oil field physician, a machinist and a newspaperman.

In the east wing we are led more deeply into the oil industry and demonstration of the manner in which oil and gas deposits were formed through the compacting of ever-changing sediments and the gradual transformation of ancient marine life into hydrocarbons under pressure and heat. Core samples polished to the gloss of precious stone provide both beauty and instruction in the manner by which differing layers of rock were formed though

millions upon millions of years. Diagrams and rock samples give us a painless lesson in the succession of the geologic ages, from the Precambrian up through the most recent past. Particularly featured are cores from the Permian Age which gave the Basin its name, for these provided many of the most important oil and gas deposits.

We come upon an assortment of drillers' hand tools from the Basin's early exploration period. We see, hear and feel a full-sized replica of a cable tool rig's drilling floor, much like that of the legendary Santa Rita No. 1. Here a walking beam moves rhythmically up and down while authentic sound effects dramatically suggest the hiss of the steam engine, the clanking and knocking, the physical vibrations caused by the strike of a bit at the bottom of the hole.

Under a "yellow-dog" lantern, full-sized wax figures depict the driller adjusting the drill string, which rises and falls in the hole, and the tool dresser heating a dulled bit in a forge so he may beat it back into sharpness with a sledgehammer. The effect is so realistic that red-faced visitors occasionally admit they have asked questions of the lifelike mannequins. Oldtime oil men have stood and watched in silence, carried back in memory through the years to similar drilling floors. Built by Q. L. "Shorty" Hall and Midland's Ford Chapman, another veteran of the early fields, this is a splendid example of the living

Cable Tool Exhibit   Staff Photo

exhibits which George Abell envisioned.

Moving beyond the cable rig floor, we see modern rotary methods represented by a large display of equipment including drill bits, among them the first conceived and developed by Howard R. Hughes, Sr. after the 1901 Spindletop discovery.

Most visitors enjoy playing the "oil game," which illustrates in an entertaining manner one of the facts the oil industry has so often tried to impress upon the public, the high-stakes gamble inherent in this ever-uncertain business. We spin a roulette-type wheel which demonstrates the cost of drilling a wildcat well. When the wheel stops, its flashing lights reveal the outcome, most frequently a total loss of our make-believe investment.

We pass through a door and suddenly find we have stepped back fifty or sixty years to a boomtown street corner of the 1925-1930 era. Here we find a barbershop,

general store, horse-powered water well drilling machine, oil field supply, theater, water pump, and even an one-horse powered rotary water well drilling machine. We pump gasoline by hand up into an old-fashioned glass-top tank. A nest of eggs reminds us that early oil field workers brought their rural upbringing and self-reliance with them. We look up on top of the barbershop porch and discover a sign painter taking a snooze after his labors, his stomach rising and falling to the rhythm of his breathing. Photographs, clothing and other memorabilia of the time are displayed inside a store. Taped voices of people who lived in Permian Basin boomtowns recall the lifestyle of those pioneering days, only yesterday in the memories of so many still living, yet vastly different from the life we know today.

A stunning highlight for most visitors is the marine diorama, which takes us back in three dimensions 230 million years to the ocean floor of the azure Permian Sea when a reef was being formed, a reef eventually uplifted by geologic forces to become the exposed face of El Capitan Peak at the western edge of the Permian Basin. The effect of standing in the ocean is uncannily real and eerie. We are carried away by the illusion of water on the other side of the huge glass. We feel a strong effect of looking down into a dark and bottomless void, and upward through the sea toward the sunlight. This singular creation, forty-feet deep and largest of its kind in the

The north wing is our last indoor area to be explored. It is the newest, built at a cost of $1.5 million and dedicated in 1981 by Vice President George Bush. Its addition enlarged the Museum's indoor exhibit space by forty percent, allowing a substantial expansion of educational exhibits, most of them dealing with the industry's production phase, getting the oil out and keeping it going.

Grabbing our attention just after we enter this wing is a dramatic blowout diorama, which demonstrates with vivid crimson visual effects and startling sound what a 1930s well explosion would have looked and felt like. A blowout, a traditional hazard in the oil field, may occur when natural high pressure that exists deep in the earth pushes oil, gas and salt water in an uncontrolled manner up through the well to the surface, where it explodes with such force that it may blow a drilling rig apart. The demonstration is so realistic that we imagine we feel the heat from the simulated explosion and the flames that follow.

An adjacent video display, using tapes of actual well fires, shows the techniques such famous firefighters as

Memorabilia Room   Courtesy, Roland K. Smith

world, took two years of labor by artist-paleontologist Terry Chase and partner George Baldwin. They molded and painted nearly two hundred thousand replicas of sea creatures which lived in that prehistoric age.

We pause in leaving the east wing and watch in a circular five-screen theater a fast-paced pictorial description of the nation's energy needs, now and in the future.

Paul N. "Red" Adair have used to bring these disastrous accidents under control. Blowouts of this nature are no longer common, thanks to technology which has produced effective means of control by mechanical blowout preventers. We find one of these devices on display. A series of four Gervasi paintings depict the famous Bill Roden blowout fire of 1968 in Winkler County, and the dynamiting, capping and cementing operations used by firefighter Adair and his crew to bring it under control.

Much of the display area in the north wing is devoted to the details of oil drilling and production, the machinery and techniques used, the high costs of completing either a dry hole or a producer. There as elsewhere throughout the Museum, audio-visual displays, models and charts demonstrate to us such practices as casing and cementing, perforating, fracturing, acidizing and separation. We find a large section devoted to pipeline construction methods of yesterday and today. We see a two-horse wagon once used for hauling pipe, its bed removed and the pipe carried atop the extended running gear. We see a sideboom tractor used in a later period for lifting, swinging and moving pipe to the ditch prepared for it by pick and shovel or by early digging machines. Greatly enlarged old photographs complement four paintings by John Scott to show us how pipelines were laid a generation and more ago.

Youngsters in particular enjoy the cutaway demonstration of a nitro shot at the bottom of a well, climaxed by a countdown and an unexpectedly strong blast that impacts the floor beneath our feet.

Another popular visual display is a patrol plane long used for rapid inspection of pipelines and a search for leaks, often easier to spot from the air than on the ground. We see suspended from the ceiling a 1948 model Luscombe 8F plane which flew more than twenty thousand hours and covered nearly two million miles in the service of Mobile Pipe Line Company. Beneath the plane, we look down at a large screen upon which a six-minute motion picture shows the continuously-moving view as it would be seen from such an aircraft flying at one or two hundred feet above ground. We follow the course of a buried pipeline across miles of Texas grasslands, sandhills, mountains and salt flats. At last we see a dark patch of ground, betraying an underground oil leak that the pilot will report by radio so a repair crew can be dispatched immediately.

A large lighted pipeline map invites us to push a button and see if our own region of the country receives a portion of its natural gas from the Permian Basin. The map reveals that Basin gas goes into homes, businesses and factories as far away as Arizona, California, the

Dakotas, Iowa, Kansas, Minnesota, Mississippi, Missouri, Nebraska and Nevada, as well as to neighboring states Arkansas, Louisiana, New Mexico and Oklahoma.

Several displays are devoted to the service and work-over operations which bring slowed or broken-down wells back into production. Cartoon character "Dr. Petro" demonstrates the various facets of this necessary element in oil field routine. Among the displays we stop to examine a 1929 "Bulldog" Mack Truck complete with winch for pulling rods and tubing out of the well hole. This six-ton chain-drive vehicle originally had solid rubber tires that rattled its riders' teeth. It saw long service in the Big Lake, Forsan, Mentone, Royalty, Westbrook and Wheat fields.

Another display demonstrates the several methods employed to produce additional oil by secondary and tertiary recovery.

A final exhibit in the north wing features some of the great variety of end products which today's consumer enjoys, often without knowing that their source is oil and gas. Displayed around a derrick we find such petrochemical articles as false teeth, plastic toys, a basketball, a styrofoam cooler, plastic water sprinkler, roller skates, plastic notebook, paint, briefcase, nylon rope, fan belt, acrylic glass cleaner, carpet, raft, backpack, fabric, nylon paint brush and fishing lure, just to dramatize the great variety of everyday items we so often take for granted.

We are told that Americans consume petroleum products at the rate of three and a half gallons of oil and more than 250 cubic feet of natural gas for a day for each man, woman and child.

Some of the Museum's best showpieces are outdoors. We examined Santa Rita No. 2 and National No. 3 as we entered the grounds. But those are only a starting place.

Behind the Museum is the Oil Patch exhibit, covering nearly two acres, dedicated to the men of the oil fields whose calloused hands dug the ditches, drilled the wells, built the tanks and pipelines, men who endured the blistering heat of summer and the bitter north winds of winter because it was their job.

The Oil Patch exhibit is the largest collection anywhere of antique drilling equipment. Eight full-sized cable tool rigs represent the gradual improvement of technology from the early part of this century to the relatively recent past.

Among the pieces are the Wichtex 18, built in Wichita Falls to be skidded from site to site; the National No. 2, forerunner of the No. 3, built about 1910-1915 and rated capable of drilling to 2,500 feet; the Fort Worth Super D Spudder, built about 1930 and usable to about 3,000 feet; the Star Drilling Machine No. 24, dating from about 1915; the Keystone Spudder No. 5½, an early portable rig meant for shallow drilling; the Star Spudder No. 49C, built about 1930 for heavier duty and deeper drilling; the Wichtex No. 66 spudder, a large machine equipped with steam locomotive-type boiler and single-cylinder Acme steam engine of a kind that powered many drilling rigs until scarcity of water and sometimes fuel caused its replacement by diesel and gas units after World War II; a casing pulling unit used in the 1930s for working over and servicing tired wells; and finally a central power unit dating back to the 1930s, a National Supply Co. Model 12-C us-

Blowout Preventer   ©H. K. Barnett

Well Fire Diorama   Staff Photo

ing an eighteen-foot bandwheel to pump as many as a dozen wells from a central location by means of moving steel rods set just above ground levels, often routed up and down or around hills. The practice declined with mandatory spacing and the development of economical individual motorized units.

Less obvious than the exhibits but important to researchers and students of the oil industry's history is the Museum's Archives Center and Library, the repository for manuscripts, documents, photos, motion pictures, letters, maps, diaries, tape cassettes and much more that

Good-Times Gusher   ©H. K. Barnett

relate to industry history. The collection of photos of petroleum pioneers, early boomtowns and oil fields exceeds six thousand. Books tracing the history of the oil industry in Texas, the Southwest and the Permian Basin, periodicals and supply company catalogs (dating back as far as 1884) graphically illustrate the advancement of oil field equipment through the years. More than six hundred tape recorded interviews of industry and boomtown pioneers will gain in value as historical treasures with the passage of years.

Whether we spend an hour in the Permian Basin Petroleum Museum or we spend a day, we come away with a richer understanding of the Permian Basin, its environment, its people and its petroleum industry which glories in a dynamic past but looks ahead toward an equally dynamic future.

THE PETROLEUM HALL OF FAME

Dedicated to Those Who Cherished the Freedom to Dare,

and Whose Work and Service Helped Build the Permian Basin.

Let Their Achievements Be Remembered

and Their Beliefs Inspire.

*T*he purpose of the Petroleum Hall of Fame, as stated in the Museum's by-laws, is:

...to honor those persons and firms who have made outstanding contributions to the development of the petroleum industry or have served as worthy examples to those in the petroleum industry, and thereby to record such examples of service, strength of character and achievement for the inspiration and education of present and future generations.

The Hall of Fame received its first member in 1968, several years before the Museum itself actually opened.

Each odd-numbered year a maximum of four people are inducted into the Hall of Fame. Those inducted have been elected by the Museum's governing boards, after an exhaustive study of their qualifications by a special committee.

Submission of names of persons, living or deceased, for election to the Hall of Fame may be made by any interested party. Candidates not chosen in the year submitted will be automatically reconsidered in future elections.

If you are interested in submitting a name for consideration for inclusion in the Hall of Fame please contact the Museum office for additional information and nomination guidelines.

GEORGE T. ABELL

Geologist, landman, independent oil and gas producer, George T. Abell of Midland, a native of Kansas, graduated from Colorado A&M College. He walked over much of Colorado, Utah, Wyoming, New Mexico and West Texas mapping structures. Going into business for himself in 1930, he spent the larger part of his working life as a wildcatter and producer in the Permian Basin. He discovered or participated in development of the Basin's Abell, Gomez, Pecos Valley, South Ward, Shipley and other fields, as well as the Grapeland gas field in East Texas. He took upon himself many civic leadership responsibilities. A philanthropist, he has shared the fruits of his endeavors with many worthwhile causes, not the least of them the Midland Memorial Hospital and the Permian Basin Petroleum Museum.

Elected 1972

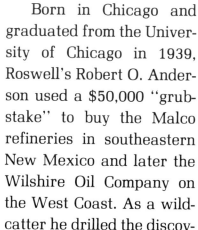

ROBERT O. ANDERSON

Born in Chicago and graduated from the University of Chicago in 1939, Roswell's Robert O. Anderson used a $50,000 "grubstake" to buy the Malco refineries in southeastern New Mexico and later the Wilshire Oil Company on the West Coast. As a wildcatter he drilled the discovery well of New Mexico's great Empire-Abo Field which brought him and his Hondo Oil and Gas Company into Atlantic Refining. He became chairman and chief executive officer of Atlantic and orchestrated the merger of Atlantic with Richfield Oil, Sinclair Oil and eventually Anaconda. As chairman of the Atlantic Richfield Board he presided over ARCO's discovery of the Prudhoe Bay Field on Alaska's North Slope. Besides his leadership in industry development, he is noted for his many philanthropies.

Elected 1982

JESSE CLEMENT BARNES

Born in Alabama, Jesse Clement Barnes was in insurance and later became involved in hotel management in Arizona. In 1936 he went to Texas to learn the oil business and a year later moved to Midland. In 1938 he drilled an important well that extended the Keystone Field in Winkler County. Later he joined with Russell Conkling in helping define the TXL Field in Ector County. After World War II he became a pioneer and advocate of deeper drilling, opening up the Emperor Deep Field in the Permian Basin in Texas and portions of the Anadarko Basin in Oklahoma. A dedicated 32nd degree Mason, he was generous with time and funds to numerous civic and public causes and active in his church. He died at eighty-three in Fort Myers, Florida.

Elected 1980

HORACE M. BAYER

Horace McDonald "Rusty" Bayer rose from surface geologist to vice president during nearly four decades with Gulf Oil Corporation. The Wisconsin native and World War I veteran earned a B.A. degree in geology in 1924 from Oklahoma University. After mapping much of West Texas for Gulf he was promoted in 1927 to zone geologist in Midland. In 1944 he was transferred to Fort Worth as chief geologist. In 1953 he became vice president in charge of the Texas and New Mexico region which yielded more than a third of Gulf's national oil and gas production. He spearheaded Gulf discoveries in Ector County's Goldsmith Field, Winkler County's Keystone Field and Andrews County's Triple N Field. Early in his career he mapped the subsurface feature upon which Gulf drilled the first Ellenburger discovery in the Delaware Basin, opening the Worsham-Bayer Ellenburger gas field in Reeves County. He retired in 1960.

Elected 1984

BEN C. BELT

Ben C. Belt was an early believer in the Permian Basin's petroleum potential and highly instrumental in its development. Born in Marshall, Missouri, and graduated in 1910 with a degree in geology from the University of Oklahoma, he spent most of his working life with Gulf Oil Corporation. As early as 1925 and 1926 he understood the key features of the Permian Basin's geology, based on the little data then available and on experiences in Mexico and elsewhere. With Lovic P. Garrett he developed major exploration proposals for Gulf and was a constructive influence in that company's taking an early and very large land position on what became known as the Central Basin Platform. The Yates, Goldsmith and McElroy fields were developed under his direction. He became a vice president of the company with offices in Houston, where he was a leader in civic enterprises. He retired in 1955.

Elected 1969

CHARLES E. BEYER

Charles E. Beyer, born in St. Louis, Missouri, started with the petroleum industry in 1907 as a tool dresser in the Mexican oil boom, becoming clerk, paymaster and a layman specialist in law. He studied geology and Spanish at UCLA, then was brought back into the oil business by his old friend, Levi Smith, with whom he had worked in Mexico for Penn-Mex, a Benedum-Trees company. In 1925 Beyer joined Smith at Texon, Texas, with the Big Lake Oil Company, also a Benedum-Trees operation. He became the company's vice president and general manager and remained so until his retirement in 1950. During a long tenure in Texon he was a civic leader, earning friendship and respect for himself and for his company. Whether the project involved law enforcement, baseball or the Boy Scouts, Beyer freely gave his time and his enthusiasm to making the community better.

Elected 1973

CLAUDE W. BROWN

Reared in Ballinger, Texas, Claude W. Brown worked for the Hughes Oil Company at Mexia, in the Currie, Wortham and Corsicana oil fields and in Brown County. He and an associate began contracting in 1928 but lost their cable tool rig in the Depression. Brown started over as a dealer in second-hand equipment. In 1935 he opened the Brown Pipe and Supply Company in McCamey and built it to six supply stores in West Texas and New Mexico. He bought salvage wells in the McCamey Field and deepened them to better pay zones. In 1951 he and geologist son-in-law, Ed W. Thorp, brought in the discovery well of the Brown and Thorp Field near Girvin in Pecos County. Brown was board chairman of McCamey's Security State Bank and a director of several important industry organizations. A promoter of education, he was presented an Honorary Doctorate by McMurry College in Abilene.

Elected 1984

PRENTICE F. BROWN

Prentice F. Brown had a knack for finding oil that earned special respect from fellow geologists. Born in Colorado, he was graduated from the School of Mines in Golden. He worked briefly for a Denver consulting firm, then for Honolulu Oil, based in California. He moved to San Angelo in West Texas in August, 1926, after discovery of the Yates and Hendricks Fields. Based later in Midland, he undertook an ambitious subsurface mapping project that resulted in discovery of the Harper, the Parker, the Bennett-Wasson, the Dugan or Slaughter and other notable fields. His name was given to the Prentice Field southwest of Lubbock. He became a vice president and director of Honolulu. After retiring from the firm, he continued working as an independent and made several more wells in the Permian Basin.

Elected 1982

RAIFORD H. BURTON

Raiford Harold Burton was a native of Magnolia, Arkansas, and attended Southern State College. He became interested in the new field of geophysics in the late 1920s and pioneered its use in the Permian Basin. After leaving Amerada Petroleum in 1946 he entered the LP gas business, but his heart was in oil exploration. He organized Burton Geophysical, later to become Burton Exploration Company, responsible for many notable discoveries including the Headlee Field. His leadership and intimate knowledge of oil exploration techniques gave his company a national reputation in the industry. His interests went beyond the petroleum industry, however. He is remembered in his chosen home city of Midland for his activity in community service, church and youth leadership.

Elected 1969

JOHN P. BUTLER

As a banker, John P. Butler earned the affection and respect of oil men in a time when few in his chosen field understood or related to the adventuresome risk-takers of an inherently hazardous industry. An associate once said John Butler was the only man he knew who never had an enemy. Under the leadership of this Mount Calm, Texas, native, The First National Bank of Midland built one of the most effective oil and gas departments in Texas and New Mexico. In 1953 he became bank president and in 1963 chairman of the board. In 1975 he was named honorary chairman. He has long been active in a broad range of civic and cultural pursuits. He was the first chairman of the Permian Basin Museum's board of executors and, with George T. Abell, brought to its creation a special wisdom, diligence and fidelity.

Elected 1975

DR. JIM CAMP

Taking healing to the ranches, the farms and into the oil fields, Dr. Jim Camp of Pecos spanned the era from horse and buggy to jet plane, from calomel to penicillin. Tennessee-born, a graduate of the University of Tennessee College of Medicine, he went to Pecos in 1900 and was the first doctor to remove an appendix in the Trans-Pecos region. He took in stride the challenge of the oil boom's tremenduous population increase. When Sid Richardson requested medical care for his people, Dr. Camp gave it even though Richardson did not have the money to pay him. Serving on the school board, he helped create the modern Pecos school system. A dedicated church man and Mason, a charter member of the Pecos Rotary Club, he helped form a six-county medical society. The Texas Medical Society named him Doctor of the Year in 1950.

Elected 1973

N. FORD CHAPMAN, JR.

Ford Chapman became interested in the artifacts of the oil field trade in his youth, when he began sketching tools and other objects around cable tool rigs. He kept alive the lore of cable tool drilling in art, in collecting and in actual use, for he made himself into one of the best-known cable tool drilling contractors in the Southwest. He drilled many wells and found important fields in Reeves and Culberson counties and elsewhere. He has been an enthusiastic backer of civic projects, especially those aimed at making the region more liveable for children and youth. Schreiner Military Institute in Kerrville honored him as a distinguished alumnus. He lent his knowledge and leadership to the Permian Basin Petroleum Museum from its beginning in 1967. He earned a reputation as a man loyal to his hundreds of friends, a man proud of his country and his industry.

Elected 1980

CARL G. CROMWELL

Carl G. Cromwell was brought up by his father to be a driller, starting in the oil fields of Pennsylvania and West Virginia. He was representative of that hardy band of drillers who tolerated grueling hardships and uncertainties, but were ready always to do their job wherever and whenever needed. Cromwell was a colorful man who liked fast cars and airplanes, who dressed smartly, talked well and was not afraid to venture. When he started a job he stuck to it. He spent nearly two years on the famous Santa Rita No. 1, drilling a little more than three thousand feet of hole. His wife and daughter lived with him in a frame shack at the location, miles from town. He kept drilling despite isolation, money and supply problems, and a perennial heavy turnover of cowboy labor. His persistence paid off when the well came in on May 28, 1923, and launched, in earnest, the Permian Basin oil boom.

Elected 1969

CAVEN J. DAVIDSON

Caven J. Davidson of Fort Worth, nicknamed "Red," was a daring, resourceful wildcatter of the legendary type. Born in Frio County, Texas, he attended Texas A & M College and saw Navy service in World War I. His oil career began during the Ranger and Desdemona booms, where he was a tool dresser, bank teller, bookkeeper and always a student of the oil business. In 1927 he began cable tool drilling, which he continued to love even after he changed to rotary drilling in later years. He believed in charting wells, which helped him become aware of Permian Basin trend possibilities. His first wildcat was brought in on the Cummins Ranch in Ector County. In 1935, with Honolulu Oil, he took a long chance in Yoakum County and brought in the discovery well that opened the Bennett Ranch Field. He was highly instrumental in development of oil and gas in the north part of the Permian Basin.

Elected 1973

MORGAN J. DAVIS

Morgan J. Davis of Houston was born in Anson, Texas, and was graduated from The University of Texas in 1925 with a degree in geology. He joined Humble Oil and Refining Company at Roswell, New Mexico, and worked there four years as a geologist. He led geological exploration in Java and Sumatra, then returned to Roswell in 1934 as district geologist and after two years was sent to the Gulf Coast as division geologist. He moved into management of Humble's exploration department and worked up to become president of the southwestern affiliate of Standard of New Jersey in 1957. When the Humble name was carried over to the new national company, Exxon, USA, that took over all of Jersey's domestic interests in 1960, he was named president. He retired in 1963 as chairman and chief executive officer. Known as a superb geologist, he was also interested in oceanography, philosophy, geography, history and charitable work.

Elected 1973

RONALD K. DeFORD

Ronald K. DeFord of Austin is both a distinguished geologist in the Permian Basin and a respected professor of geology at The University of Texas at Austin. Born in California, he received two degrees from the Colorado School of Mines in 1921 and 1922. From 1923 to 1933 he did pioneering work in the Basin as a geologist for Midwest Refining Company. He joined Argo Oil Corporation in 1933 and soon was chief geologist with an office in Midland. He studied the surface and subsurface geology of Colorado, Utah, Kansas, Wyoming, New Mexico and Texas and was instrumental in locating the Hobbs Field discovery well, among others. He led many geologic field trips sponsored by the West Texas Geological Society, which he served as president. He turned to education in 1948 to share with others what he had learned. He has received many professional honors and he is active in civic leadership.

Elected 1975

FLOYD C. DODSON

Floyd C. Dodson of San Angelo was a geology pioneer in the Permian Basin. Despite the loss of an arm in a boyhood hunting accident near Eden, Texas, he was active in sports and vigorously pursued his chosen career after earning his degree in geology from The University of Texas at Austin in 1920. He studied the geology of Reagan and adjoining counties long before the Santa Rita No. 1 discovery and strongly shared the conviction of Big Lake attorney Rupert Ricker that oil existed in the area. He and Ricker established one of the largest and most active geologic firms in the Basin, representing ten large companies and doing studies in fourteen counties. Their recommendations were a strong factor in the Basin's development. Dodson shared his expertise, hiring young geology graduates to do field mapping. He trained several to positions of industry leadership, to carry on his traditions after his death at fifty-three.

Elected 1975

HIRAM M. DOW

Hiram M. Dow of Roswell was an attorney who contributed much to the orderly development of the oil and gas industry, helping create New Mexico's comprehensive oil conservation acts. Born in Cotulla, Texas, he lived most of his life in Eddy and Chaves Counties of New Mexico. After receiving his law degree from Washington and Lee, he set up practice in Roswell and in 1937 and 1938 served as lieutenant governor of New Mexico. He was instrumental in formulating the 1929 and 1930 state laws that permitted the commissioner of public lands to approve prorating and well-spacing agreements. He later assisted in obtaining interpretations of these laws by New Mexico courts. He aided in formation of the Oil Compact Commission and represented his state on it for twenty-two years, until 1958. He was always a leader in the betterment of his community, Roswell.

Elected 1969

HERBERT B. FUQUA

Herbert B. Fuqua, nick-named "Babe," had a long career in oil, followed by another in banking. He managed, financed or inspired no fewer than fifteen field discoveries and twenty-three major extensions in the Permian Basin. Born in Indian Territory, he earned a geology degree from the University of Oklahoma and joined Gulf in 1922, first in Wichita Falls, then San Angelo and Fort Worth, ultimately heading its southwestern operations from Houston. In 1949 he became board chairman and chief executive officer of Texas Pacific Coal and Oil Company in Fort Worth. He became a chairman of the board of Fort Worth National Bank in 1952. After Texas Pacific's assets were sold in 1963, he turned full attention to banking. More than half of the $250 million in oil venture loans made during his active service as chairman went to the Permian Basin.

Elected 1973

LOVIC PIERCE GARRETT

Lovic Pierce Garrett was a pioneer oil man, born in LaGrange, Georgia, and brought to DeLeon, Texas, when he was twelve years old. He studied geology at The University of Texas, was graduated in 1902 and joined the old Rio Bravo Oil Company. By 1908 he was a member of Gulf Oil's Houston organization. He was named president of the American Association of Petroleum Geologists in 1931. He introduced seismologists from Germany into this country. He was instrumental in persuading Gulf to drill what became the first commercial oil well producing through a salt dome overhang. In 1924 he added torsion balance and seismograph parties to Gulf's exploration department and pioneered in the application of these methods outside the Gulf Coast. He worked closely with Ben Belt and others in developing a major position for Gulf in the Permian Basin. He was a Gulf vice president at the time of his death.

Elected 1969

BERTE R. HAIGH

Berte R. Haigh, born in Los Angeles, had only five months of high school yet somehow qualified for a degree in mining engineering and geology in 1925 from what is now The University of Texas at El Paso when he was thirty-five. He had done farm work, peddled gasoline, worked as a garage mechanic, raced automobiles and had seen military service on the Mexican border and in France. He worked in his chosen profession two years, was on the UTEP faculty six years as assistant professor of geology and engineering, and in 1934 transferred to The University of Texas Lands System as staff geologist, then came to Midland as geologist-in-charge. He developed or assisted in developing many oil and gas leasing techniques later adopted by public agencies here and abroad. He constantly promoted exploration and new secondary recovery techniques. During his tenure the UT endowment grew by more than $500 million.

Elected 1972

ERLE P. HALLIBURTON

Born in Tennessee, Erle P. Halliburton left home at fourteen to work and support his widowed mother and five brothers and sisters. He spent five years in the Navy before World War I, taking up the study of engineering and hydraulics. In 1916 he joined the Perkins Cementing Company of California, and the diagnosis and care of wells became his lifelong career. In 1920 his firm became the Halliburton Oil Well Cementing Company — now the Halliburton Company — and began making technical innovations still recognized as among the industry's major accomplishments. His crews and equipment went everywhere from Algeria to Zanzibar. His name was known from the Permian Basin to the jungles of Java and Sumatra. He extended his leadership from industry to widespread civic endeavors and philanthropy. He was a self-made man in the true tradition of Horatio Alger.

Elected 1982

OLIVER C. HARPER

Oliver C. "Kip" Harper, educated in geology at the University of Chicago, flew for the United States Air Corps in World War I and took up geology as a profession in Kansas and Oklahoma with what is now Cities Service. In 1922 he joined Gulf Production Company in Sweetwater, when the Westbrook Field in nearby Mitchell County had produced but little and the subsurface configuration of the Permian Basin remained mostly unknown. Using existing wells, Harper and colleague Ernest Closuit began attempting to solve the Basin's geological mysteries. In 1924 Harper finished one of the most significant pieces of geological evaluation yet seen: the recognition and delineation of the Central Basin Platform. Many fields resulted from his work. Later, as an independent, he was responsible for the Harper and Foster fields, for interesting Amon Carter in drilling the Wasson field discovery well and for at least six other field discoveries.

Elected 1972

HOUSTON HARTE

Newspaper publisher Houston Harte followed the growth of the Permian Basin's petroleum industry with daily coverage in his flagship publication, the *San Angelo Standard-Times*, giving encouragement in print and sometimes in a financial way to exploration and development. He and his staff consistently covered the oil fields, starting with a Mitchell County discovery in the early 1920s and a Westbrook barbecue celebrating a first railroad shipment of oil from that county. His newspaper was on hand to report in detail Reagan County's Santa Rita discovery and the rapid extension of exploration which followed in Upton, Crane, Pecos, Winkler and other counties. His hallmark was prompt, accurate and objective reporting of news. Through his many effective political ties he worked behind the scenes to provide a favorable climate for growth of the oil and gas industry and of West Texas.

Elected 1969

THOMAS S. HOGAN

Thomas Stephen Hogan, born near Chippewa Falls, Wisconsin, spent most of his early life in Montana. An attorney, he became Secretary of State for Montana in 1896 and was elected to that state's Senate in 1914. In later years he held federal offices in Washington. He was also a rancher and investor. In Midland in the late 1920s and early 1930s he foresaw the migration of oil operations and companies into the Permian Basin. He participated in the sale of the McElroy Ranch properties of Upton and Crane counties to the Franco-Wyoming Oil Company and in other significant transactions. He invested a large part of his personal fortune in Midland, going against much advice to construct a twelve-story building which at first bore his name and for years was the tallest such structure in West Texas. It became a magnet, drawing oil company offices and industry talent to Midland and bearing out the validity of his dream.

Elected 1969

EUGENE HOLMAN

Eugene Holman of Monahans was graduated from what is now Hardin-Simmons University in Abilene, gained a master's degree in geology and joined the Humble Oil organization in 1919. He was among the talented young geologists tutored at Humble by Wallace Pratt, and he rose steadily within the world's largest oil company, Standard Oil (New Jersey). He played a key role in development of the firm's large Venezuelan production and ultimately became board chairman and chief executive officer. Nevertheless, he always thought of himself first of all as a professional geologist. He contributed many technical papers and remained deeply interested in oil exploration throughout his career. Even when his duties took him far away, he returned each year to the Permian Basin and kept close contact with family and old friends, always living up to his Texas upbringing.

Elected 1969

HOWARD R. HUGHES, SR.

The rock bit conceived and developed by Howard Robard Hughes, Sr. sped the development of the Permian Basin's oil and gas industry. Born in Keokuk, Iowa, Hughes studied law at Harvard and the University of Iowa and practiced awhile in his hometown before going into lead and zinc mining in Joplin, Missouri. Hearing of the Spindletop discovery near Beaumont, he went to Texas, took some leases and found some oil. Rotary drilling was limited by the old fishtail bit, shaped like a turning chisel, which did poorly in rock. In 1908 Hughes and business associate Walter Sharp modeled a bit made up of two cone-shaped toothed cutters. By 1914 it had been used in 11 states and 13 foreign countries. The Hughes Tool Company was formed in Houston. Continuing to improve on the original design, Hughes poured work and imagination into the merchandising of his bits but died before he could realize the magnitude of his contribution.

Elected 1973

HERBERT C. IRVIN

In a sense, the Hall of Fame honor given to Herbert C. Irvin includes his father, William Howard "Vinegar Bill" Irvin, and his brother, William Irvin Jr. The elder Irvin was born in Titusville, Pennsylvania, the first Capital of Oil, in 1871. In 1910 he was drilling in Oklahoma. By 1916, when the oil tide was moving west of Fort Worth, he was in the Breckenridge Field. By the time he contracted to drill five miles west of Colorado City in 1920, his two sons were old enough to join him on the cable tool rig. Their well was dry. Father and sons worked on many exploratory wells drilled by Steve Owen and Sam Sloan, including the big well that opened the Dora Roberts Ranch Field near Big Spring. "Bert" Irvin also was involved in the Owen-Sloan well that found the Chalk Field in Howard County and on many in Scurry and other West Texas counties. In 1927 he left drilling and went to Oklahoma City, joining a savings and loan association.

Elected 1972

PAUL KAYSER

Paul Kayser saw the potential in natural gas when most people still regarded it as an unwanted by-product of oil. Born on a farm near Tyler and educated at Baylor University, he studied law by correspondence from The University of Texas and practiced in Houston. By 1928 he was convinced that gas was a marketable commodity and founded the El Paso Natural Gas Company, then set about creating outlets. When conservation of gas was forced on the petroleum industry, El Paso provided markets and prevented massive shutdowns of oil wells. The clean fuel helped El Paso's Arizona and California markets manage their air pollution problems. El Paso also opened up new uses for gas as a raw material for chemicals in the Permian Basin. Kayser was board chairman and chief executive officer of his firm from 1928 until 1965. His leadership created markets and jobs, and he lent his talents to many industry organizations.

Elected 1973

FRANK H. KELLEY

One of the best-remembered of the Permian Basin's great landmen is Frank H. Kelley of Colorado City. A native of Washington County, Indiana, he attended Indiana University, Indiana State and Columbia University and served the Navy during World War I. He landed in Colorado City in the early days of the Permian Basin's oil boom and never left. As division staff landman, he served Magnolia Petroleum and its successor, Mobil Oil, for 38 years until retiring just before his death. He was given tremendous trust and allowed to use his own judgment in cases involving huge sums of money. He was largely responsible for Magnolia's extensive position in Mitchell and Scurry counties. The Kelley-Snyder Field was named for him. He headed the Texas Good Neighbor Commission, directed the West Texas Chamber of Commerce water program and served as the group's president. He was a rancher and, on his own, a successful oil man.

Elected 1973

HAYMON KRUPP

Haymon Krupp of El Paso was one of a handful of visionary men brushed by fate in the form of a single oil well: Santa Rita No. 1. Krupp, at the time of this landmark discovery, was already a successful merchant and manufacturer, having gone to El Paso at age sixteen in 1890. He was nearing fifty years of age when he accepted an opportunity to invest in and lead the Santa Rita venture. He became president of Texon Oil and Land Company, shouldering the difficult and initially uncertain task of handling the company's financial affairs. His encouragement and his ability to find money for land and drilling made it possible for Frank Pickrell, Carl Cromwell and others to bring in that most famous of wildcat wells and launch the petroleum industry's great push into the Permian Basin. He remained a valued civic leader in El Paso and is long remembered for many quiet philanthropies.

Elected 1969

EDWARD A. LANDRETH

Edward A. Landreth of Fort Worth was once described as a man who had the character to withstand both disaster and outstanding success. He knew both. Born in Springfield, Illinois, he spent most of his youth in Joplin, Missouri, and entered a family-owned mining machinery company. He went to the Breckenridge Field in 1919 to sell machinery, fell in love with the oil business and built one of the earliest gasoline plants there. He sold that and other holdings in 1924 and by 1926 had drilled sixty wells before selling to Phillips Petroleum. In 1927 he embarked on a long career of oil discovery in the Permian Basin and was associated with such fields as the Hendricks, Taylor-Link, Penwell and Hobbs. He was also active on the Gulf Coast. He was an early campaigner for oil and gas conservation, a role which in 1954 won him the Distinguished Service Medal from Texas Mid-Continent Oil and Gas Association.

Elected 1972

E. RUSSELL LLOYD

El Capitan Peak at the far western rim of the Permian Basin fascinated geologist E. Russell Lloyd, native of West Virginia. While a Rhodes Scholar at Oxford he vacationed in the Alps and other European locations where geological formations intrigued him. His career included work with the United States Geological Survey, with Sinclair Wyoming, with Roxana Oil in Roswell, with the Superior Oil Company in Midland, and as an independent geologist. He sensed that El Capitan Peak was part of a great reef system which formed the western boundary of a sedimentary basin. His studies of this reef system and of limestone problems in geological interpretations led to his becoming an internationally recognized authority in his field. His colleague, John Emery Adams, once called him the foremost geologist in West Texas. He was associate editor of the American Association of Petroleum Geologists *Bulletin* for years.

Elected 1978

ARTHUR M. LOCKHART

Arthur M. Lockhart was one of the earliest marketers of Permian Basin oil. With his brother, Lloyd E. Lockhart, he organized Rio Grande Oil Company in El Paso in 1915. Brothers Cecil, Herman, Leslie and Lynn also joined the enterprise at various times. They first sold gasoline and kerosene in El Paso, then opened a refinery there. Expanding, they bought refineries in Phoenix and Los Angeles, their assets eventually becoming part of today's Atlantic Richfield. In 1922 the Lockharts opened the Basin's first pipeline, twenty-nine miles long, to move oil from new wells in Mitchell County. There is also reason to believe they took delivery on two tank cars of oil from an even earlier Mitchell County well as far back as 1917. In the early years of Basin expansion they provided one of the few outlets for its oil. In later years Arthur Lockhart became a processor of asphalt in Long Beach, California.

Elected 1972

DEAN E. LOUNSBERY

Dean E. "Cap" Lounsbery came to know the geology of the Permian Basin as few others did. A 1919 graduate of Cornell University, he spent a year on the faculty, then did geological work for Whitehall Petroleum Corporation in western India, Baluchistan and Burma. He did field work from 1922 to 1924 for Midwest Refining in the Panhandles of Oklahoma and Texas, in the mountain states and the Permian Basin. He was district geologist for Midwest in Abilene two years, then district geologist for Phillips Petroleum in San Angelo, laying the foundation for much of that company's Basin reserves. In 1933 he went to Bartlesville, Oklahoma, becoming chief geologist for Phillips in 1937. From 1952 to 1962 he was technical assistant to the vice president of the land and geological department. A major contribution was Phillips No. 1 Glenna in 1952. He was also involved in acquiring large lease holdings in the Goldsmith and Embar Fields.

Elected 1972

RALPH F. LOWE

The energetic Ralph F. Lowe of Midland participated in the drilling of at least five hundred wells in twenty-five years. Born in Lewis County, Missouri, he attended Westminister College at Fulton. He worked briefly for a hotel in Casper, Wyoming, then joined Oil Well Supply. He worked in Kansas and Oklahoma and in 1927 was a machinist in Wink, Texas. He became a shop foreman, then a service station operator in Midland and a marketing consignee, all the while picking up a broad working knowledge of the oil business. In 1940 he contracted to drill his first well on the Seth Campbell lease in Winkler County and in 1941 bought his own cable tool rig. By 1943 he had drilled twenty-five wells in Winkler County. He was heavily involved in the Fullerton play and found extensions of the Denton and Gladiola Fields of Lea County, New Mexico. He played a major role in oil activities in Andrews County, the Coyanosa Field in Reeves County and the Indian Basin Field of Eddy County, New Mexico.

Elected 1973

CHARLES V. LYMAN

Charles Vernon "Cap" Lyman was one of the Permian Basin's most successful wildcatters and producers, having what others felt was an almost magical ability to see prospects in the mesquite and greasewood flatlands of West Texas. Left fatherless when young, he attended the University of Virginia and Sewanee and served in World War I. By 1921 he was in the Texas oil business. His overflowing energy led him to open important fields in Winkler and other West Texas counties as well as in South Texas. He was a true early conservationist who sought to save and use the tremendous amount of gas produced by his own wells when flaring was still the normal practice. He had a wide-open personality, loved laughter, athletics and music. He was a generous donor to the Midland YMCA, to West Texas Boys Ranch and many other worthwhile causes. He died in Phoenix.

Elected 1980

GEORGE B. McCAMEY

George B. McCamey of Fort Worth had the distinction of seeing a West Texas town named for him without his having lived there. His sixty-two-year connection with the oil business included countless wildcat wells. Born in Pennsylvania, he worked as a boy cleaning old oil wells, then became a roustabout and tool dresser and owned his own string of tools while still a very young man. He pioneered with the oil industry in Illinois, Oklahoma, Louisiana, Utah, Montana, South Dakota, Kansas, Kentucky, New Mexico and Texas. In 1925 he began drilling the M. L. Baker No. 1 in Upton County. The Orient Railroad put in a switch nearby and stationed a boxcar labeled McCAMEY. The town which grew up around the switch took the name. He sold his properties to Atlantic Refining Company in 1943 but continued to drill wildcat wells until his death. His many philanthropies included a quiet program for helping old and penniless drillers.

Elected 1975

ERNEST W. MARLAND

Ernest Whitworth Marland was a dynamic innovator who knew both prosperity and loss. Born in Pittsburgh, Pennsylvania, he acquired a law degree from the University of Maryland in 1898 and worked with Guffey and Galey, a pioneer oil firm, while he learned geology. He found his first oil in West Virginia in 1906, then lost his first million in the Panic of 1907. He put surface mapping parties to work in the Permian Basin in the mid-1920s and was instrumental in several major discoveries. Marland Oil was an aggressive developer of the fields near Wink. He imported seismic methods of exploration from Germany in 1921, an interest shared with Gulf, and formed what may have been the first oil company research organization. He relinquished control of his firm when it merged with Continental Oil Company in the late 1920s. He took up a new career in politics, was elected to Congress and became governor of Oklahoma.

Elected 1978

JOSEPH C. MAXWELL

Joseph C. Maxwell of Fort Worth was Kentucky-born and gained his first oil experience with the Prairie Oil and Gas Company in Kansas. Starting as a landman, he began to acquire leases on his own account. He was in the Ranger boom and took leases in Howard County in 1921 after the Westbrook Field discovery. He and his brother, David Maxwell, were in South Texas when they heard about the Santa Rita discovery in 1923. He tried but failed to acquire the McElroy Ranch leases, then in 1926 was a key figure in discovery of the Church-Fields-University portion of the McElroy Field. His success led him into Crane, Ward and Winkler counties of West Texas and into Lea County, New Mexico, as one of the outstanding independent producers. In 1951 he was involved in discovery of the five-pay West Dollarhide Field. He was a founder of the Texas Independent Producers and Royalty Owners Association and was generous to worthy civic and philanthropic causes.

Elected 1975

STANLEY C. MOORE

Stanley C. Moore demonstrated his energy and ambition while attending Rice University in the late 1930s. He flew on Sundays with the National Guard, took a correspondence course on being an officer, managed the Rice bookstore, worked at night for Houston's electric company and managed to court the young woman who was to be his wife. He took a cut in pay to become an engineer with Hughes Tool. He made a career of listening to rig hands' complaints and suggestions, then finding the technology that would solve their problems. In 1952 and 1953 he founded and named Drilco, a company serving the technical needs of the oil industry. He inspired that firm with his traits of service and hard work and took those same characteristics to Smith International when Drilco was incorporated into it. It has been said that ideas he brought to the industry have saved it hundreds of millions of dollars.

Elected 1980

ROBERT W. PATTESON

Robert W. Patteson began scouting the Permian Basin from Midland when Gulf Oil established its district office there in 1926. In early Fords and Dodges, he managed somehow to cover his wide territory over endless miles of poor roads, carrying his own water, patching tires, often driving at night. Sometimes stepping around rattlesnakes, he knew how to count through fieldglasses the strings of pipe in a "tight" well to learn at what depth a wildcat was drilling. He was representative of the best of the oldtime oil scouts, reflecting credit upon his company and earning a wide respect for his knowledge and ability. Widely-known, well-liked, he became also a landman, staff coordinator, banker, public relations officer and constant supporter of civic affairs. He retired from Gulf in 1959 and from Commercial Bank and Trust in 1964, just before his death.

Elected 1975

NEVILLE G. PENROSE

Neville G. Penrose of Fort Worth was one of the Permian Basin's aggressive wildcatters. A native of Philadelphia, he first came to West Texas in 1928 and began operating independently in 1932. One of his most noted discoveries was the Cary No. 1, drilled in 1935 in what became known as the Penrose Field, later consolidated with the Skelly Field. He found important Texas fields in Andrews and Upton counties as well as New Mexico's Drickey Queen Field in Chaves County and Brunson Ellenburger Field in Lea County. He earned a reputation as a successful entrepreneur and energy-seeker. He also was acclaimed for his service in the cause of international understanding. Labeling himself a grassroots diplomat, he served as chairman of the Good Neighbor Commission in an effort to improve and maintain good relations between his own country, Mexico and Central and South American nations.

Elected 1975

FRANK T. PICKRELL

Frank T. Pickrell's name will always be associated with the legendary Santa Rita No. 1 well. He helped find financing for it, hired Carl Cromwell as driller for it, and found markets for the oil that came from it and later nearby wells. Born in Ennis, Texas, he was a successful businessman in El Paso before service in Army Intelligence during World War I. A chance encounter with a former army colleague on a train led him toward his place in Permian Basin history. Rupert Ricker of Big Lake told him and Haymon Krupp of exploration permits on University lands. Pickrell and Krupp acquired the permits and set out to raise additional funds. Theirs was the rankest of wildcats, drilled on a shoestring, far from known production, even named for the Patron Saint of the Impossible. Pickrell later admitted that he did not know what an oil well did or looked like before the Santa Rita was drilled.

Elected 1968

WALLACE E. PRATT

Wallace Pratt of Tucson was long associated with Humble Oil. Born in Phillipsburg, Kansas, he received his bachelor's and master's degrees in geology from the University of Kansas. He became Humble's first geologist in 1918 and was in charge of the company's geological work until 1928. Subsequently he held various management jobs, became a director, member of the executive committee and finally a vice president of Standard Oil Company (New Jersey). It was largely under his leadership that Humble became a very large factor in the Permian Basin. He did the original geological work that led to the Bronte Field. The reef problem in the Guadalupe Mountains was addressed by Humble geologists under his active interest and encouragement. He did much to elevate the profession of petroleum geology.

Elected 1969

SID W. RICHARDSON

Sid W. Richardson was one of that rare breed of wildcatters who wrote oil history through daring ventures others would not undertake. Born in Athens, Texas, he attended Hardin-Simmons University and Baylor but left school for the oil fields. He was at Ranger and Burkburnett, then made his first Permian Basin discovery in the Keystone Field in Winkler County. He was involved in development of the Slaughter Field and, in 1956, in Winkler County's Halley Field. He had close ties in Monahans and Kermit. He undertook natural gas and carbon black ventures in West Texas, moved his wildcatting into Louisiana, acquired a Texas City refinery, and held a premier patent position in the development of underground storage in salt formations. He was in ranching, radio and politics. Before he died, he placed most of his assets in a philanthropic foundation.

Elected 1969

JAMES T. ROBISON

Remembered for his farsighted administration of public school lands, James Thomas Robison was a native of Cass County, Texas. He served thirty years in the Texas General Land Office, first as a clerk, next as chief clerk from 1900 to 1908, and finally as commissioner, an elected position he held for twenty years, until his death. His administration was marked by a sincere regard for both the people who bought the lands and the state's financial welfare. His plans for lease sales of land, for governing mineral operations on state lands and for regulating payments to state school funds and The University of Texas are now an integral part of West Texas development and prosperity. A teacher, a legislator, an 1899 graduate of The University of Texas Law School, he lived to see his plans for proper handling of school lands confirmed into established land law by the Texas Supreme Court.

Elected 1969

ROBERT W. RUSSELL

Robert Warwick Russell was born at Parker's Landing, Pennsylvania, the son of a Scotsman who had opened his own machine shop in 1879. At thirteen Bob Russell left school to learn his father's trade. Later, in Burgettstown, Pennsylvania, the Russells helped build the first gas engine that powered a drilling rig successfully. Soon they were manufacturing them. Another shop was opened in 1905 in West Virginia. In 1935 Bob Russell opened a machine shop in Monahans, Texas. He and his people labored over steam equipment and welded stems for drilling contractors, often working twenty-four hours a day to keep badly-needed machinery in operation. In 1966, after three generations had served the oil and gas industry more than eighty years, the Russells sold their Monahans shop, and Bob retired.

Elected 1969

WILLIAM G. SKELLY

William Grove Skelly was the son of an oil teamster, so the sights and sounds of drilling were part of his boyhood experience. Born near Erie, Pennsylvania, he learned about oil at Oil City, in that state, and began a long and remarkable career as an industry pioneer, philanthropist and civic leader. He struck his first oil at age twenty-six, carrying out an early ambition to build an oil business of his own. He wildcatted wherever oil play was to be found. He was a large factor in such legendary Texas booms as Electra, Desdemona, Burkburnett and Ranger. His Skelly Oil Company helped create the great fields of Winkler County and influenced development elsewhere through one of the region's larger field offices. He integrated his company vertically, making it a giant in Texas, Oklahoma, Kansas and elsewhere. It later became a major part of Getty Oil Company's domestic operations.

Elected 1978

HAZEN P. SLAGEL

Hazen P. "Cap" Slagel was involved in drilling from boyhood, when he helped his father produce brine wells near his birthplace at Mason City, West Virginia. Slagel was a Wells Fargo messenger in Atascosa County, Texas, a captain with the 36th Division, worked in the Ranger oil field and arrived in Colorado City in 1919. He worked as a tool dresser or driller on many important Mitchell County wells. These, together with an earlier flurry far to the west around Toyah, brought the first oil industry interest to the Permian Basin. He was on the Morrison No. 2 well, second and best of the early Westbrook Field producers in 1922. He was involved with the Sloan-Miller No. 1, which extended the Westbrook. He was on the Chalk No. 1, which opened the Chalk Field in Howard County. As an independent producer he was involved in the Ira Field in Scurry County and wells on the Foster Ranch near Iatan.

Elected 1972

SAMUEL A. SLOAN

Samuel A. Sloan was a pioneer in two great fields, oil and aviation. Raised in Altus, Oklahoma, he was a World War I combat flier for the Army Air Service and developed a love for flying. In 1919 he went into the oil business at Colorado City, drilling a deep 4,008 foot hole on the Landers Ranch. It was dry. In the early 1920s he shared in a series of significant wells with Steve Owen of Tulsa and others. He drilled some alone, including the Chalk Field discovery well in 1926 and an early major well in the Dora Roberts Field in 1926-1927. He drilled one of the first wells in Loving County and many in Mitchell, Reeves and Taylor counties. He was instrumental in establishing the first airports at Fort Worth and Midland, the latter named for him. He was working on establishment of a Fort Worth-El Paso commercial service when he died on January 1, 1929, in the crash of his own plane.

Elected 1972

LEVI SMITH

Levi Smith was a pivotal figure in development of the Big Lake Oil Company and was founder of Texon, Texas. Born in West Virginia, he was associated with early Benedum-Trees oil interests in Illinois, Louisiana and Mexico. As their emissary he traveled worldwide, to Columbia, Venezuela and Romania. He went to Desdemona, Texas, when Transcontinental Oil Company was organized in 1919. After Santa Rita No. 1 began flowing in 1923, he spent several weeks studying its performance, then persuaded Benedum-Trees to participate. As president of Big Lake Oil he began a vigorous drilling campaign, moving his family to West Texas. He chose the Orient Railway boxcar site of Texon as the town for his employees and their families. He built a model community, the first company town or camp in the Permian Basin. He was responsible for the Yates Field discovery well, known as the Queen of the Pecos, in 1926.

Elected 1984

FRED TURNER, JR.

Fred Turner, Jr., of Midland, was born on a ranch in Coleman County, Texas. In his youth he dressed tools and learned about drilling. In April, 1927, he went to Midland as a scout for Marland Oil Company. He found what he believed to be a vacancy in Pecos County's Yates Field. The primitive nature of early-day surveying had left scattered unsurveyed lands. He drilled on the vacancy in 1933, after classic litigation, and brought in a big producer. He pushed ahead with a discovery in Lea County, New Mexico, the West Lovington Field. He made other discoveries in Andrews County, the Shafter Lake San Andres, the Parker Wolfcamp and Parker Pennsylvania Fields. He was active in Ector and other Texas counties as well as San Miguel County, Colorado. Boyhood memories took him into the ranching business, where he raised fine cattle and thoroughbred horses. He was on his Brownwood pecan farm when he died.

Elected 1975

CHARLES D. VERTREES

Charles D. Vertrees' productive life paralleled the Permian Basin's oil development. Born in Linn County, Kansas, he moved with his family to the Texas border and was graduated from high school in Brownsville in 1918. To finance his college education he worked as a truck driver in Mexico's oil fields. He received a degree in geology from The University of Texas in 1923 and returned to Mexico as a geologist for East Coast Oil Company. In 1925, in San Angelo, he was hired as a paleontologist by Marland Oil Company, which later merged with Continental Oil. In 1929 he was moved to Midland as district geologist. He served the company from 1926 until his retirement in 1958 as regional research geologist. He and Continental were credited with such fields as the Todd Ranch, the Elkhorn Ellenburger, the Wasson and the Slaughter. He served as president of the West Texas Geological Society and authored that group's history.

Elected 1984

VAN S. WELCH

Van S. Welch of Artesia, New Mexico, drilled his first well at the turn of the century in Allegany County, New York, where he was born. Later, with Thomas Flynn, he drilled the discovery well of Wyoming's Elk Basin Field. He drilled in Illinois and at Burkburnett in Texas. In the 1920s, with Tom Flynn and Martin Yates, he undertook three wells in the Pecos Valley near Artesia, New Mexico, selling acreage to raise money and promising the drilling crew part payment in oil. The third of the wells was the successful Illinois Producers No. 1, completed June 29, 1924. It opened up the great southeastern New Mexico fields. Welch and his partners were chief instruments in enlarging the Permian Basin's production toward its westward limits. He remained a citizen of Artesia, establishing college scholarships for students in each of Artesia's three major ethnic groups.

Elected 1969

WILBUR A. YEAGER, SR.

Wilbur Arthur Yeager, Sr., is said by some to have been the first oil man to come to Midland to live, back in 1926 when it was a city of some three thousand people and almost that many windmills. Born in Alexandria, Missouri, he attended the University of Missouri and served as a military flyer in World War I. Just after the war he signed on with Prairie Oil and Gas in Oklahoma. He later worked with Sinclair and then went into the ranks of the independents. His partner in the quest for oil was James M. Armstrong, himself a distinguished geologist and engineer. In one way or another Yeager was associated with most of the worthwhile developments in Midland from the time he moved there with his bride to participate in the growth of the Permian Basin's oil industry.

Elected 1975

MICHAEL L. BENEDUM
JOSEPH C. TREES

One an operating man, driller and engineer, the other a specialist in financing wildcat ventures, Michael L. Benedum and Joseph C. Trees were an ideal partnership. Products of a pioneering 1890s West Virginia oil boom, they discovered major fields in Illinois and the Caddo Lake Field in Louisiana. They found oil in Canada, Colombia, Mexico, Romania, Venezuela and Texas. In late 1923 they were instrumental in organizing the Big Lake Oil Company that developed Big Lake oil field after Santa Rita No. 1 blew in. In 1926 conventional wisdom held that oil could not be found west of the Pecos River. Nevertheless, Benedum and Trees, in joint venture with a firm that would become Marathon Oil Company, endured a disappointing series of dry holes in Pecos County and gambled on the Ira Yates Ranch 60 miles from known production. The Yates Field became one of the greatest finds ever made in the U.S., thanks to these bold men who brought the frontier's adventuresome spirit into a new century.

Elected as a Team 1969

RAY V. HENNEN
ARTHUR M. HAGAN

As a team, Ray V. Hennen and Arthur M. "Jack" Hagan were largely responsible for two vastly important occurrences in Permian Basin petroleum history. Under a work assignment from West Virginian Hennen, the Pennsylvania-born Hagan selected and recommended to famed wildcatter Mike Benedum the development of the Big Lake oil field following the Santa Rita No. 1 discovery. Again under instructions from Hennen, Hagan spent ten long months during 1923 and 1924 leading a geological survey party over a strip of land a hundred miles long and twenty miles wide from Emerson in Terrell County to Stiles in Reagan County. He found a promising structure feature and recommended a test well. Hennen, having faith in Hagan, passed on the recommendation to Benedum and Transcontinental Oil Company. The result was the Ira G. Yates discovery well. The two men worked together only a short time, but nevertheless set great events into motion.

Elected as a Team 1975

EARL G. RODMAN, SR.
WILLIAM D. NOEL

A unique and lasting partnership between Earl G. Rodman, Sr. and William D. Noel was sealed by nothing more than friendship and a handshake. It has created enormous good for the city of Odessa and for the Permian Basin. Noel, after early wildcatting, bought into Earl Rodman's supply company, and the two began a successful career in oil exploration over the Southwest. They went into the gasoline plant business as Odessa Natural Gas Company. In 1956, after years of groundwork, they launched the petrochemical complex in southeastern Odessa that created hundreds of jobs and pumped much-needed revenue into the city's economic lifelines. They branched into banking, ranching and a multitude of other enterprises. They were also involved in civic-improvement programs that enhanced the lives of their fellow West Texans.

Elected as a Team 1982

ARCH H. ROWAN
CHARLES L. ROWAN

The Rowan brothers, Arch and Charles, grew to young manhood at Alvin, in East Texas, roughnecked for Humble Oil and learned to appreciate the sweet scent of oil at Mexia. In 1923, when the Powell Field boomed near Corsicana, they formed Rowan Drilling Company. It became one of the largest drilling firms, a pioneer in technology and outlook. It was one of the early firms active in the Permian Basin, especially in the Wink and Big Lake areas. A sister company, Rowan Oil Company, was formed in 1948 and moved with speed and imagination into the Basin and other parts of the Southwest. Its assets later became a major part of the Texas Pacific Coal and Oil Company. Rowan Drilling was transformed into Rowan Enterprises, Inc., of Houston and became a major international drilling company. The Rowan brothers settled in Fort Worth, giving their time and money to many good causes.

Elected as a Team 1978

THE PETROLEUM MUSEUM

1500 Interstate 20 West • Midland, Texas 79701 • 915/683-4403

July 7, 1988

Ms. Betty J. Tate
5511 Del Cerro Blvd.
San Diego, CA 92120

Dear Ms. Tate:

Thank you for your membership donation of $1,000 to the Petroleum
Museum. Your support enables us to educate the public about oil
and gas, to preserve and explain our heritage, and to continue
expanding our educational programs for children and adults.

Your complimentary admission tickets will be kept on file at the
Museum. (When you wish to use them, or let friends or family use
them, just ask at the museum office upon arrival.)

Enclosed you will find your Sustaining Member membership card
which entitles you to a 10% discount on purchases made in the
museum gift shop.

We look forward to seeing you in the museum during the coming
year and at the workshops and programs we will be offering. Your
contribution is greatly appreciated. As a way of saying thank
you for your generous gift, please accept, with our compliments,
this copy of our book, PERMIAN: A Continuing Saga. In addition,
you will receive a one-year subscription to Southwest Oil World
magazine.

Sincerely yours,

Edward C. Rowland
Executive Vice President
Director

ECR/ds
Encs.